"We all at some point on life's journey experience heartbreak, loss and grief. Perhaps you are facing it right now in your life or you know someone who is. If so, this book is for you or that someone.

Ruth encou[illegible] her teenage years and later, [illegible] ivileged to have known Pe[illegible] ample of a man of faith a[illegible] d Saviour, Jesus.

Ruth's beau[illegible] the reader to feel, know a[illegible] break and grief. She writes from her heart, being open and honest, yet always seeking her Lord's help, guidance and will. Her gift of writing is profoundly and divinely inspired, which takes you to another level of joy and victory in Christ Jesus, who promises to never leave or forsake us, but to be with us always."

Pastor Ryan Morton, Keynsham Elim Church

"I lost my wife in 2020 and can identify so readily with Ruth's journey. She writes beautifully and compassionately, communicating deeply the pain and vulnerability we feel at such times. This book is a great witness to believers going through the pain of loss.

I love the way Ruth has woven it all together through the metaphor of the birds, underpinning everything with Scripture. I so wish it had been available to me in 2020!"

Dr Roger Greene, Director of Tricordant

Through Grief to Triumph

Ruth Raby-Elmer

ISBN 978 1 73933 120 7
e-ISBN 978 1 73933 121 4

First edition 2023

Acknowledgements

Cover design © Clair Lansley

Printed in the UK

A catalogue record for this book is available from the British Library

In honour of my husbands,
Jean-Paul Raby and Peter Elmer,
who were dedicated to me and our children.
They are the reason this book was written,
and they will forever be in our hearts;
missed for a short while
but reunited in eternity.

Contents

Contents

Introduction

I distinctly remember God speaking to me on the morning of the 28th of October 2021. It was a Sunday and I was sitting in bed having my quiet time. I asked him to share what was on his heart, and as I waited I heard my heavenly Father speak out Proverbs 3:5-6:

Trust in the LORD with all your heart
and lean not on your own understanding;
in all your ways submit to him,
and he will make your paths straight.

With that passage of Scripture came a quiet whisper, "You need to write your story."

The thought had never entered my mind before, but suddenly the challenge was set before me. I asked God to confirm his word through someone else and left it at that. I got up, dressed and went to church.

After the service, I bumped into two ladies who were chatting outside. We were having a short conversation when one of the ladies, Zynia, unexpectedly said, "You need to write a book."

BOOM! She provided the voice of confirmation I had asked for. It could not have been any clearer, and it arrived on the day of asking.

Given the choice, my desire would have been to write a testimony of God's miraculous healing, but this was not to be the case as I had lost two husbands to ill health: Jean-Paul in 2002 and Peter in 2021. I know that both are home in glory now and completely healed, which brings me great comfort, but instead of a testimony, God invited me to write a book about the events that occurred in the year after Peter's passing; an unveiling of the journey he took me on through the valley of weeping between April 2021 and April 2022. It was a journey of healing and restoration, and through it I experienced a deeper work of the cross.

I have also written this book as a legacy for my children: Rachel, Luke, Samuel, Jessica and Ben. I am proud of them all, especially for the fortitude and courage they have shown after losing their father. In fact, Rachel, Luke and Samuel have lost two fathers. Memories of these two wonderful men will remain with us throughout our lives, and we take comfort in the fact that they are at home in a far better place. I cannot wait for the welcome party when we are all reunited. I can picture them now, willing us on and encouraging us to keep our eyes fixed on Jesus, the pioneer and perfector of our faith (see Hebrews 12:2).

It feels as though death has been following me all my life. My father died when I was nineteen and then both husbands passed away, so I have known the depths of pain and heartache that bereavement brings. However, I have also encountered God in these times. He has shaped my life and deepened my foundation in him, strengthening me throughout the process.

Grief and loss are life-changing events that ripple out and catch everyone in their wake. Grief is an unavoidable part of life. Jesus said that he came to give abundant life (see John 10:10), and the Bible tells us it is the blessing of God to live to a ripe old age (see Isaiah 46:4) However, we know that this is not the case for everyone. Losing a loved one at any age brings sorrow, but when there is an untimely death we feel robbed, realising how fragile, cruel and short life can be. The tragedies and losses we experience remind us that we live in a broken world; that God's original plan for humans to live eternally on earth has become marred by our sin.

At the time of writing this book, Russia is at war with Ukraine. The devastation we have seen on the news, and hearing about all the people who have needlessly lost their lives, forces us to question what is life all about. It makes us realise that our days are but a breath (see Psalm 39:5), but we also know that Jesus has offered us eternity with him. This is good news! John 3:16 says that "whoever believes in him shall not perish but have eternal life. I'm looking forward to the day when I see my Saviour and am reunited with my loved ones; the day when I, too, enter my eternal rest.

In April 2021, God began to speak to me in a new way through the introduction of five birds: the sparrow, the raven, the dove, the swallow and the eagle. I have always loved God's creation, and I'm so thankful that he found it fitting to use these winged creatures to teach me and demonstrate his love to me.

In the valley of grief, God spoke words of revelation into my life. I experienced visions that I have been careful to give an honest account of in this book. I have felt the pruning shears and the heat of God's refining fire, cleansing and healing my heart. His desire is for us to walk in victory, persevering through our grief, but he wants us to experience his comfort in our suffering as well.

My journey through grief was not one of inactivity or wallowing, although both happened on occasion. It was mostly the opposite; I went into overdrive. I felt the urge to keep moving forward. This was my positive stance! I was determined not to let grief get the better of me, although the pain I felt was beyond words.

This is not just a book about grief; it is a testimony declaring the goodness and triumph of God. The good news is, we always win in Christ because he overcame all the obstacles and trials of our earthly life when he died on the cross. All he asks is that we trust him during the recovery process.

God is not the *giver* of pain, but he is the *answer* to it. No one would ever choose to walk this road, but for me it became a place of dependence on God, as all other distractions fell by the wayside. This was the place where he did his greatest work of transformation in my life. At times, grief has made my life feel dark, empty and ugly, but I have also experienced the beauty of life through God's comfort and healing, As Ecclesiastes 3:11 says: "He has made everything beautiful in its time."

If you are experiencing grief, my hope is that you will find encouragement and comfort as you read this book, knowing that God is with you. He loves you and is committed to restoring you. He will carry you through this dark, painful time, and I pray that you will encounter his tenderness, grace and love-filled presence. Don't give up on God. Choose to trust him in your pain. For in your darkest moment will come the dawning of a new day.

Chapter One

The Prophecy

In his hand are the depths of the earth,
and the mountain peaks belong to him.
(Psalm 95:4)

I still remember the carefree days of my twenties, when life was uncomplicated and there was a promise-filled future there for the taking. Back then I was working for the TV Licensing company in Bristol. I often headed out of the office during my lunch hour to take a breather.

On one such day in 1990, I strolled across to the Debenhams cafeteria. The place was quiet and half empty; just what I needed to unclog my mind from the busyness of office life. I had been sitting there for no more than five minutes when a grey-haired lady approached and asked if she could join me. I agreed, but I felt a little bemused and uneasy given that there were plenty of unoccupied tables nearby.

It was then that the lady placed a magazine on the table. Instantly recognising it, I commented, "Oh, you have a *Prophecy Today*! You must be a Christian."

"Why, yes," she replied. "God told me to come and sit with you."

She had my full attention. She introduced herself as Thirza and we chatted for a while. Within a few minutes she had invited me to her home the following week. I was intrigued, to say the least. It was most definitely a God-ordained meeting, and I knew that I should accept her invitation.

A week or so later I spent an afternoon sipping tea and eating lunch with Thirza at her beautiful country cottage. I sensed she was a woman of wisdom, having gained great experience and knowledge through a life well lived. My own life was at a crossroads, and I anticipated that I would receive a word of direction through her.

She asked if we could pray, and I agreed. After a while, Thirza began to share a picture she had seen in her spirit of me on a beautiful sunny day, standing in the cool shade of some trees at the bottom of a hill. She said that there would come a time when I would climb that hill, but that I would do so in stormy weather. She hinted that I would meet someone and that we would make the ascent together.

I wasn't sure what to make of it all, and I didn't like the thought of climbing a hill in a storm. It wasn't the best word I could have received, but I decided that, if it were from God, all would become clear in time.

Before I left, I asked Thirza what God was doing in her life. She replied, "I'm in the cleft of the rock. Here to do God's will."

I didn't fully understand her words at the time, but have since come to understand that she was referring to Christ: our hiding place, our rock of safety.

I thanked her and left the cottage. I never met Thirza again, but her words remained with me. Unbeknown to her, they put the wheels in motion for my future. Those fleeting encounters impacted my life greatly, and I look forward to being reunited with her when we reach our heavenly home.

The map and the compass

Not long after I received this prophecy, a book called *Hinds' Feet on High Places* by Hannah Hurnard (Kingsway Publications, 1982) came into my possession. This book is an allegory of the Christian life and is about becoming more mature in one's faith. The character named Much Afraid is called up from the valley to the heights by the Shepherd and has to learn how to leave her earthly problems behind. It really mirrored the story of my life in the years that followed and became a road map of God's word in guiding me.

Around the same time, I was listening to an album called *In the Stillness* (Integrity Music, 1990) by Christian songwriter Chris Bowater. I was particularly captivated by "The Sovereign Lord", the lyrics of which are based on Habakkuk 3:19, which says:

> *The Sovereign LORD is my strength;*
> *he makes my feet like the feet of a deer;*
> *he enables me to tread on the heights.*

I finally had the map (the book), and the compass (the song) to point me toward my destination. As I let all this soak in, I felt so drawn to the call of "the heights", although I didn't really understand what that meant at the time.

Reaching the peak

As I thought about the prophecy, I was perturbed by the idea of scaling a mountain in stormy conditions but felt confident that I would experience joy when I reached the peak. It evoked memories of the life of adventure I had embarked on at sixteen, when I participated in the Duke of Edinburgh Award. I learned expedition skills, including how to use a map and compass to navigate the countryside and mountainous regions. I then went hiking in the Lake District with a group of other teenage girls so we could put our new skills into practice.

I will never forget the long ascent up one mountain when the weather conditions were not in our favour. The cold, driving rain pelted our bodies, hampering our progress. There were moments when we felt the strong desire to give up, yet we spurred one another onwards and upwards, singing songs to keep our strength up and our morale high.

Overcoming the elements made our victory all the sweeter, and we were rewarded with great joy when we reached the summit. There is nothing quite like the glorious feeling of triumph as you gaze down at the world spread out beneath your feet. All our hard work and perseverance had paid off. It was worth the pain of every blister and aching limb for the elation we experienced when we realised we had conquered the heights. We had never felt more alive than at that moment when we found ourselves standing on the mountaintop.

God's saving grace

However, it was on this same mountain that I nearly lost my life. There was a horrible moment when I slipped and tumbled off a ridge. I thought my life was about to end, but I quickly realised I had somersaulted onto a lower ledge, with my backpack taking most of the impact of my heavy landing. Below me was a sheer drop to the valley. Praise God that I lived to tell the tale.

As I look back over my life, I have seen the hand of God intervene on many occasions. There will always be spiritual mountains to climb and valleys to walk through in our Christian lives. My comfort is that we have a loving Father who, like my teenage friends, is watching over and encouraging me to keep moving towards the finish line.

It's important to remember that mountains and valleys are interconnected. You can't have one without the other. And the deeper the valley, the higher the mountain. The valley may be a place of green pasture, bringing refreshment, peace and restoration. But it can also be a place of shadow and darkness. Spiritually, mountains can be tough to climb, but they can also be places where we encounter God. I have had a few of those.

In the Bible, the mountain of the Lord represents his rule and authority. When the Israelites were to enter the Promised Land, the Lord spoke to them, saying: "But the land you are crossing the Jordan to take possession of is a land of mountains and valleys that drinks rain from heaven. It is a land the LORD your God cares for; the eyes of the LORD your God are continually on it" (Deuteronomy 11:11-12).

It was also a land of giants; enemies that had to be fought and overcome. However, God promised to give the Israelites victory if they walked in his ways. And he kept his promise, as he always has with me – both on the mountain and in the valley.

Trusting God

Mountains can harbour hidden physical dangers, and in the spiritual realm there are mountains of illness, pain and grief that need to be cast down, along with the devil, who opposes the work of God. But in all the ups and downs of life, God walks with us. He simply asks us to trust his leading as we take hold of his hand. We must remember that it is in the trials of life that we really grow spiritually. At our most difficult times we come to understand that our own strength and wisdom is futile, but that God's strength and wisdom will never fail us.

My experiences of mountains have afforded me a healthy respect for them. As a result, I approach them with the caution and reverence they command. Whenever I look up at a mountaintop I think of the greatness of God, and of his majesty and wonder. I often reminisce about those days of adventure with my friends, and how we conquered the heights despite the difficulties we faced. Those adventures instilled in me a resilience that undergirded my life for what was to come.

The prophecy Thirza had spoken over my life implied that I was about to be taken on an uphill journey in stormy weather. I had no idea what would take place, but I knew that it would change the course of my life. I never would have chosen this path, yet I know that it was the right one because of the people who came into my life as a result and enriched it with their love.

Reflection

God has the best plan for your life, and he will lead you in the way that you should go. I pray that you would trust him, knowing you are part of his wonderful story. He has good things in store for you. Embrace the adventure!

Prayer

Thank you, Lord, that you have a good plan for my life. I ask you to show me how I fit in with your purpose, and I look forward to seeing where you will lead me. Amen.

Chapter Two

The Journey

Blessed are those whose strength is in you,
whose hearts are set on pilgrimage.
As they pass through the Valley of Baka,
they make it a place of springs;
the autumn rains also cover it with pools.
They go from strength to strength,
till each appears before God in Zion.
(Psalm 84:5-7)

Jean-Paul

Within a year of receiving the prophecy, I met my first husband, Jean-Paul Raby, at a house church in Bristol in 1991. I loved his open heart and warm personality. He had many gifts and talents, one of which was playing the guitar. He often recorded his own music.

We were married within a short space of time and children followed very quickly. Rachel and Luke were born within the first two years, then Samuel a couple of years later. Our family felt complete, and bringing up three little ones was wonderfully busy. We felt as though we were on a journey as a family, with

God leading us every step of the way. Psalm 84, including the verses at the start of this chapter, was a portion of Scripture that spoke clearly into our lives at this time, and in the darker days that were to come.

Jean-Paul's work as an IT consultant allowed him to be based at home, which enabled him to spend lots of precious time with the children during their formative years. By this time we were attending a new church in Bath. New friendships were formed there, and the children grew spiritually and socially within a fun and safe environment. Every year we spent a week of our holidays attending a Christian camp in Peterborough, hosted by Kingdom Faith Church in Horsham. These camps were full of fun, and we enjoyed plenty of happy times as we met with other families and gathered for inspired teaching and worship.

A devastating diagnosis

It was during our seventh year of marriage that Jean-Paul was diagnosed with chronic myeloid leukaemia. He wasn't panicked by the news, and our life continued fairly normally. However, a year later there were subtle changes in his ability to work, and we were alarmed that he was beginning to show signs of memory loss.

He eventually went for tests, and a scan revealed that his brain was shrinking. It was a form of dementia that didn't fit the normal pattern. The doctors were perplexed, and as there was no treatment Jean-Paul's health deteriorated rapidly.

It was hugely distressing to witness the husband I had once known become completely unrecognisable, and tears of desperation filled my prayers. One night as Jean-Paul slept I slumped onto the floor, crying out to God to heal him. It was silent and dark, and no answer came.

Within a short space of time our life had fallen apart. With Jean-Paul gravely ill and me having to care for three young children singlehandedly, it became overwhelming. On one occasion I took to my car in anguish, wailing loudly as the pain of grief hit full force.

Laying down my life

By this time it had been ten years since the prophecy, but it came straight back to the fore of my thinking at this time, as did the Much Afraid character from *Hinds' Feet on High Places*. She met with great opposition from the enemy as she heard the call of the Shepherd to the heights. It was a difficult ascent, fraught with danger, but it was when she laid down her life in full surrender that she was made strong.

The pages of that book echoed into my desperate circumstances, and I understood what was required of me. I poured my heart out to God and gave him everything: my husband, my children, my home. It was then that I heard him tell me to lay my own life down. I released all to God.

Life was so tough that it was easy to let go in that moment and surrender all. Something broke within me as I saw in my spirit what looked like a metal bar snap in half. I immediately sensed a new freedom, and I was filled with an overwhelming love that I had never experienced before. I encountered God's resurrection life filling my whole being and a new strength rose up within me. I had no idea until then that the Christian life could be so glorious.

In the days that followed, tears of heartfelt thanks flowed as I thought of the suffering and affliction Christ had endured for me on the cross. I came across these words in Isaiah 53:3-5:

> *He was despised and rejected by mankind,*

a man of suffering, and familiar with pain.
Like one from whom people hide their faces
he was despised, and we held him in low esteem.

Surely, he took up our pain
and bore our suffering,
yet we considered him punished by God,
stricken by him, and afflicted.
But he was pierced for our transgressions,
he was crushed for our iniquities;
the punishment that brought us peace was on him,
and by his wounds we are healed.

These words cut deeply into my heart, giving me a deeper appreciation of Christ's saving grace. It brought release from the power of sin over my life on many levels. I heard God say that I was "accepted in the beloved" (Jesus), and that his favour was upon me.

I had been bitterly aware of my many shortcomings. My heart was always striving to do what was right, but therein lay the problem. All of a sudden I was bathing in God's love and the power of his abundant life. It felt like a new day with a newfound peace. I truly discovered that the cross is the only way to freedom, and that it opens the way into his glorious kingdom.

The Valley of Baka

Although God continued to pour out his love, Jean-Paul's health rapidly deteriorated and he went home to glory in August 2002. We had only been married for ten years, but he had given me three wonderful children. I see his character, his gifting and his talents in all three of them.

I mourned Jean-Paul's passing, but God's powerful love carried me through that tough time and enabled me to be strong for my children. I really understood how his love could conquer all things – even grief.

Psalm 84:5-7 particularly spoke into my life at that time:

Blessed are those whose strength is in you,
whose hearts are set on pilgrimage.
As they pass through the Valley of Baka,
they make it a place of springs;
the autumn rains also cover it with pools.
They go from strength to strength,
till each appears before God in Zion.
(Psalm 84:5-7)

"Baka" means "weeping". The Valley of Baka is a place of difficulty and hardship, which is why it was given its name. Most people would not choose to go through this valley, yet those who hunger and thirst after God will undoubtedly pass through it at some point in their Christian journey. It is comforting to know that even in the valley there is provision for pilgrims via the place of springs and autumn rains, and that we will go from strength to strength as we pass through it.

I understood the autumn rains to be showers of God's love and blessing, which would give me the strength to continue. The challenging time during Jean-Paul's illness had really pushed me up against a wall and caused me to cry out to God. I learned to run to him as my strong tower in a way that I never had before, and it became a milestone of growing up in my faith. Problems that had once weighed heavily on me became easier to overcome as I was able to see more clearly through the lens of God's love.

Jean-Paul and I had journeyed through life together, ascending that stormy hill mentioned in the prophecy given to me by Thirza, until our lives took separate paths. God had taken my husband home, but my path was to continue in this life. I had three little ones who needed all the love I could give now that their dad was no longer around.

Reflection

Death reminds us that life on earth is temporary. I pray that you would grab hold of each day and be thankful for every precious moment you have to spend with your loved ones. May you dance and celebrate all the good things God had blessed you with, and may you walk into a future that is greater than your past.

Prayer

I give you thanks, God, for the precious gift of life. May I not waste any time while I am here on earth. Give me purpose and focus to walk into the future, with you at the centre of all that I am and do. Amen.

Chapter Three

Peter

I said, "Oh that I had the wings of a dove!
I would fly away and be at rest.
I would flee far away
and stay in the desert;
I would hurry to my place of shelter,
far from the tempest and storm."
(Psalm 55:6-8)

Three years had passed since Jean-Paul's death, and I had moved to Keynsham Elim Church, close to my home. This was where I met Peter, and we married in 2005. Peter was such a ray of sunshine. It was impossible to miss him. He had such presence, and his smile lit up every room. He was great fun to be with and had a touch of mischief about him. A mechanic by trade, he was creative with his hands and had good carpentry skills. Peter loved to do a job well and always made things to the best of his ability.

We became a blended family of seven, with my three children, Rachel, Luke and Samuel, and Peter's two from his first marriage, Jessica and Ben. Our hands were certainly full with five children in a house that was bulging at the seams, but Peter's sense of humour made life fun. He loved Rachel, Luke and Samuel as if they were his own, and I was really thankful they had a father figure in their lives.

Peter and I were so happy that our lives had converged. His love and support were unshakeable, and over the years our faith and love for each other richly matured. In the later years of marriage we supported a number of adults with learning difficulties in our home. One young man named Ryan lived with us for five years. It was rewarding to see his social skills develop as he became more independent.

Another devastating diagnosis

It came as a huge blow when Peter was diagnosed with pancreatic cancer in 2019 and we were told it was terminal. He was given six months to live, but despite the doctors' prognosis we continued to believe in our healing God.

During our prayer time one day, Peter had a picture of a modern-day fishing trawler going out to sea on the high waves. Like Peter the disciple, he believed God was telling him to go fishing for people. His daily walks through the park became the best fishing ground. He connected with people easily, and whenever the opportunity arose he would talk about his faith.

Peter lived well and embraced life every day. He had an amazing inner strength and peace, which clearly demonstrated God's grace in his life. He lived for two years after the diagnosis, carrying on in relatively good health for the most part. It was only in the last two months that his condition deteriorated. The weekend before he died, he saw all his family and closest friends.

Peter went to sleep peacefully at home one Sunday

afternoon and never woke up. He went home to glory at 9 a.m. on Monday 9th March 2021, after we had been married for sixteen blessed and fulfilling years. His parting left me bereft.

Shortly after Peter's death I came across a book he had recently read. In it, he had highlighted some sentences about God's rescue. It brought me comfort to know what he had been thinking about during his last days on earth. I remembered him saying that he felt like he was on the sinking Titanic, but that he would remain standing right to the end.

I thought about Peter the disciple walking on the water to Jesus. When he saw the wind and waves he was afraid and began to sink, but he called out to Jesus to save him. Jesus immediately held out his hand of rescue. With tears rolling down my face, I knew that Jesus had reached out his hand to my Peter. He had rescued him and taken him home.

Springs of living water

Grief hit hard as I was confronted with the Valley of Baka a second time. I knew all too well the pain and heartache it would bring, and I didn't want to face the road ahead. The shock of Peter's passing initially made me feel isolated and numb; even cut off from God. Like the psalmist, I cried out:

> *My soul yearns, even faints,*
> *for the courts of the Lord;*
> *my heart and my flesh cry out*
> *for the living God.*
>
> **(Psalm 84:2)**

How could this be happening again? I couldn't comprehend it. I wrestled with the "why?" question for many days and weeks, until I had exhausted every avenue and eventually surrendered.

I had to accept that knowing why would not change the circumstances of what had happened. What was important was the present, and how God was going to step into my devastating loss. Like the first, this second bereavement removed my lid of security, exposing me to the reality that I was not in control. Only God could hold my life together.

Like a tree stripped bare in the depths of winter, so was my soul laid bare before God. I sought him with all my heart, looking for answers that would satisfy my thirst. My attention was drawn to Psalm 84:5 once again, but this time to particular words that I had not fully understood at first about the pilgrims making the Valley of Baka a place of springs. I realised that springs come from under the ground, and that the ground represented my heart. Digging would be required to find the source of the water, and my roots would need to go deeper into God.

I called out to him to shine his spotlight into my life. I pressed in to him and searched out his word. I needed to find God amid all the adversity I was facing, and it was in the valley that God spoke a word into my life. He visited me with revelation, and refreshed and enlightened my understanding. He led me to those springs of living water, only for me to find that they had been blocked up. Through the immense shaking I had felt from losing Peter, a piece of neglected ground in my heart had become exposed, revealing what had been hidden in my life for a long time. I knew I needed to cooperate with God in all that he was about to do if I wanted those springs to come forth.

Full circle

It felt as though my life had come full circle, and I was deeply troubled. In fact, this valley was even deeper than it had been the first time I became a widow, and my grief was all-consuming.

I was trying to make sense of it when I heard God say, "You have come full circle, but it is not what you think. The circle is spiralling upwards."

These words encouraged me, as I understood that this valley would take me to a higher place. I could see that the deeper the valley was, the higher the mountain would be. It is the same with bereavement. There is a progression in our grief; a walk of recovery in which time eases the pain and lessens the tears, lifting the grieving soul out of its grip. My valley of weeping became a place of exposure, of humbling myself, and I knew that God was going to uncover the things in my life that needed those springs of living water and required his cleansing, healing touch.

I was inspired by Psalm 24:3-4:

> *Who may ascend the mountain of the LORD?*
> *Who may stand in his holy place?*
> *The one who has clean hands and a pure heart.*

God has always been the answer in the difficulties and trials of my life. He is my safe haven in troubled times. I was fully ready for him to have his way in my life. I knew that I couldn't continue unless he did what needed to be done.

In the book of Samuel, Hannah understood the importance of running to God in prayer. She was in the valley of tears when she faced a future without children. She wept, feeling deeply troubled and downhearted, but she also drew on the blessing of God through prayer. She sought after him, pouring out her deep need for an answer.

And she got what she wanted! She came out of the valley of tears in the course of time and bore Samuel the prophet. As she declares in 1 Samuel 2:8:

He raises the poor from the dust
and lifts the needy from the ash heap;
he seats them with princes
and makes them inherit a throne of honour.

Reflection

Your prayers will rise up from the ash heap, and you will receive what you have been asking for in time. Your valley of weeping is not a place of permanence, but a temporal place to pass through. The lessons you learn will transform your life and strengthen your faith. Hosea 2:15 talks about the Valley of Achor (trouble) becoming a door of hope. Your grief will become your door to the future.

Prayer

Lord, may I not lose sight of you in my grief. I choose to press in to you, to pursue you, until I am fully satisfied by you. Amen.

Chapter Four

Time for Tears

Blessed are those who mourn,
for they will be comforted.
(Matthew 5:4)

A few days had passed since the funeral and thanksgiving service for Peter's life, and my children had really stepped up to the plate, taking care of the house and my needs. They were amazingly strong and supportive. It felt strange to see them supporting me at first, having been their carers up to this point, but I was so proud of the adults they had become. They, too, were coming to terms with the loss of their father, but just being together was a comfort for us all.

Wider support came from other family members and friends. Many of them rallied around, providing meals and other support. I knew we were all being upheld by the prayers of many, and to this day I am thankful.

At the beginning of April 2021, my friend Tina suggested we drive to Portishead to walk my dogs, Pearl and Dime, along the coastal path to the marina. Breathing in the fresh sea air and feeling the warmth of the sun on my face would have been a good tonic had I not felt so knotted up and numb inside. I was emotionally paralysed, shut away by my pain. It was all I could do to put one foot in front of the other.

It felt like I was engulfed in fog, and I don't remember much about the walk until we reached the far end of the marina and crossed the main road to Waitrose. As we approached the supermarket, an elderly gentleman began to sob uncontrollably. A friend was embracing him, and I instantly knew these were tears of grief. I felt the man's pain in the pit of my stomach.

Tina had disappeared into Waitrose, while I waited outside, and I couldn't stop staring at the man. I wanted to help, but I knew it wasn't appropriate. Eventually, the grieving man departed and his friend walked across. He felt the need to explain.

"I'm sorry about that," he said. "His wife died last night and it was very unexpected. Poor Peter will be lost without his wife."

"Sorry, did you say his name was Peter?" I interjected.

"Yes, that's right. He's really going to miss his Ruthie."

The shock of his words hit me at full force, and I fought hard to hold back the tears. In disbelief, I questioned the man again. "Did you say that their names were Peter and Ruth?"

He affirmed it. Peter had just lost his wife Ruth.

The dam burst and tears poured down my cheeks. I blurted out that my name was Ruth and I had just buried my husband, Peter. The poor man was stunned into silence, while I was a blubbering mess.

Tina returned from Waitrose at this point to find me distraught, crying in front of a stranger. It was a bizarre meeting, but I knew that it was a "God-incidence". I asked the man to convey my condolences to his bereaved friend, then we parted company and went on our way.

The following morning I walked the dogs up to the fields near my house. The events of the previous day played repeatedly on my mind, magnifying my pain. I longed to feel Peter's hug and his reassurance that everything would be all right.

I approached a thicket of hawthorn bushes in full white bloom, and on entering I suddenly had a vision and saw my Peter. His face was lit up with his beautiful smile, and he gave me the biggest embrace. I wept as I felt his joy at seeing me again. It was a brief encounter, yet tangibly real. Then Peter handed me over to Jesus and I fell into his loving arms in deep sorrow. It was a defining moment, nailing the reality that I was no longer a wife but a widow, although it would take time to come to terms with the fact.

This was the beginning of many months of tears that followed. Looking back at these two God-incidences, I realise they were trigger points that began to unlock all the pent-up trauma and pain I had been feeling. God stepped into my grief and initiated the process of healing.

God's safety blanket

Pentecost Sunday, the 23rd of May 2021, marked just over two months of life without Peter. I travelled into Bristol with a friend to attend her church. Covid restrictions were in place, so we had to wear face masks during the service, but it felt refreshing to visit a church where no one knew about my bereavement. I wanted to meet with God; nothing else mattered.

As the gentle, anointed worship flowed, I raised my hands to receive. I felt a warm liquid spiralling up from my feet and around my body. Keeping my eyes closed, I began to see feathers falling over my head. I knew it was the Comforter, the Holy Spirit, wrapping me in his safety blanket. I thought of the verse in Psalm 91:4:

He will cover you with his feathers,
and under his wings you will find refuge.

I was enveloped in God's peace. The worship continued for a while, and then the pastor got up on stage and said, "Someone here has recently been bereaved and the Holy Spirit wants to minister to you."

The tears began trickling at first, and then became a stream. After that came the deep, uncontrollable sobs of sorrow. A lady came and prayed quietly by my side, and for several minutes I poured out my grief. It came in waves – periodically easing, only to return. Eventually the tears subsided and peace returned. I was so thankful that the praying lady didn't feel the need to interrupt, but allowed the Holy Spirit to gently minister his comfort.

The Father's embrace

Four months to the day Peter had died, I walked the dogs up to the fields with a heavy heart. I took a path through the woods, sobbing as I remembered his passing at 9 a.m. on the 9th of March. Thoughts plagued my mind as to why I had lost two husbands. I suddenly remembered my dad, who had died when I was nineteen. He had provided well for our family, but my sadness lay in the fact that I had no memories of any meaningful conversations between us. He wasn't a nasty man; he was just quiet and not very tactile.

Why did they all leave me? I wondered. I*s there something wrong with me? Why, God, did you not heal Peter?* I felt as if God had abandoned me when I needed him the most. It was then that the voice of Jesus echoed in my mind when he cried out: "My God, my God, why have you forsaken me?" (Matthew 27:46).

The anguished cry of Jesus as he bore the Father's wrath for our sin is difficult to comprehend. In the closing moments on the cross he entrusted his suffering, his pain, his abandonment – even his own life – into the Father's hands. What utter darkness. It's hard to imagine the agony of the cross, but it was all endured for humankind.

My own abandonment seemed insignificant in comparison, but these words revealed something important that I could easily have dismissed. I needed to surrender my grief into the hands of Jesus, for he had already borne it on the cross and overcome it.

Then I heard a gentle whisper: "Start talking to me as your Father."

Something profound dawned on me at that moment. I always spoke to Jesus, but rarely did I relate to God as Father. From that day forward I talked to my heavenly Daddy, picturing him with his arms outstretched. I knew I could rely on his love to keep me safe. He delighted in his daughter, and the time had finally come for me to know what it meant to be Daddy's girl.

Trusting simply as a child, and knowing the love and protection of my Father's embrace, became a refreshing road of freedom as I surrendered all. God stepped into the void to fill all that I had missed from my human father as well as the love I was missing from my husbands.

It had taken forty years of being a Christian to come to this point of realising that my constant feeling of abandonment stemmed right back to my childhood years. It was a deep-seated wound that had been hidden and overlooked all my life. It wasn't insignificant, it was major, and it had become an inroad that the devil was using to rob me. God had uncovered the source of my trauma and enabled me to take back that stolen ground. He had unblocked the well so that Christ's healing stream could fill the void. I can only say that God does everything in his perfect timing. In his great wisdom he gave me the capacity to process my grief and the pain that came with it.

A time to weep

The book of Ecclesiastes says that there is a time and a season for everything:

> *A time to weep and a time to laugh,*
> *a time to mourn and a time to dance.*
>
> **(Ecclesiastes 3:4)**

The season of tears was fully upon me. I didn't want it, but I quickly realised that my healing hinged on the natural and necessary grieving process. There was no way of getting around this; it had to be faced head-on. My world as I knew it had ended abruptly, and I was stuck in a bubble of sorrow and isolation.

I cried most days for about five months. It still amazes me that our bodies have the capacity to produce so many tears. Mornings, evenings and weekends were the worst times. Not having my best friend to share my life with was completely unbearable. The house was gravely empty, echoing the loneliness I felt.

Everywhere I went I saw reminders of Peter: in my daily walk up to the fields with the dogs and in the familiar faces of the people we met. I would suddenly see his smile or remember his laugh and it reduced me to tears, yet I knew deep down that these tears would provide the release for my pent-up feelings.

There is a Jewish proverb that says: "What soap is for the body, tears are for the soul." Tears are God's gift to us; a natural response to pain that brings cleansing and healing. Simply put, nothing makes us feel better at times like this than to cry, cry and cry some more. Crying deeply means we have loved deeply and feel the pain deeply. The parting of a loved one is the worst pain ever, and we should never feel the need to apologise for our tears.

Sacred tears

Psalm 56:8 (NLT) says:

> *You keep track of all my sorrows.*
> *You have collected all my tears in your bottle.*
> *You have recorded each one in your book.*

I am strangely comforted by these words, which reveal God's tender nature. It tells me that my tears are precious to him and do not go unnoticed. My tears of grief are sacred; spilled for the loss of a love joyously celebrated.

King David, who wrote this psalm, shed many tears. I love his honesty and vulnerability in the struggles he encountered. He didn't have his life neatly up together and looking perfect. I could relate when he was downcast in his soul, saying:

> *My tears have been my food*
> *day and night.*
> **(Psalm 42:3)**

And:

> *All your waves and breakers*
> *have swept over me.*
> **(Psalm 42:7)**

The psalms allowed me to be true to my own feelings of grief. I could connect with them personally and open up my heart to God, just as David had done. They also brought comfort and hope, knowing God was always with me even when I didn't feel him close.

I didn't think I would ever recover from the unsettling waves of sorrow that came crashing in, the force of which took me to the ground. However, this spiritual baptism became an acceptable part of my life, a daily occurrence, that somehow made me feel better. They were painful tears, but they also brought healing. Having the courage and freedom to face our feelings in grief rather than burying them is the beginning of a healthy road to recovery. Opening up our hearts in surrender is to discover the vast and never-ending tide of God's love.

David didn't hide from his pain. He ran to God, saying:

> *Pour out your hearts to him,*
> *for God is our refuge.*
>
> **(Psalm 62:8)**

We have a Father who can handle all the issues of the heart. He takes our grief, including our complaints, and shoulders the burden of them. In return, he gives us his comfort and love.

Jesus knew and related to the heartache of human sorrow. According to Isaiah 53:3, he was "a man of suffering, and familiar with pain". His response was one of compassion as he wept over his own people when they rejected him as their Messiah. Jesus also wept at the tomb of Lazarus, even though he was about to raise Lazarus from the dead. He was also deeply moved and troubled in his spirit when he saw his mother, Mary, and the crowds weeping at the cross. He felt their pain because he loved them.

I began to see more of God's compassion through my own tears, and I was saddened by and became more sensitive to other people's pain. That first encounter with the grieving man outside Waitrose struck to the very heart of my own grief. It was his pain, mingled with my own, that triggered the tears.

Jesus said:

> *Blessed are those who mourn,*
> *for they will be comforted.*
> **(Matthew 5:4)**

I have thought about that verse often, wondering why this is the case. I see now that, in a world where grief is an unavoidable part of life, it is a blessing to know and experience comfort and love, and to have the privilege of offering solace to others. As 2 Corinthians 1:3-4 says:

> *Praise be to the God and Father of our Lord Jesus Christ, the Father of compassion and the God of all comfort, who comforts us in all our troubles, so that we can comfort those in any trouble with the comfort we ourselves receive from God.*

Not only does Jesus show compassion to those who are grieving; he also gives us his resurrection life. "Jesus said to [Martha], 'I am the resurrection and the life. The one who believes in me will live, even though they die; and whoever lives by believing in me will never die. Do you believe this?'" (John 11:25-26).

He demonstrated the power of these words by raising Lazarus from the dead. Therefore, we know that death does not have the final say. This is the reality for every believer who has died and passed through into eternal life. Death has no hold over us because our lives are in Christ, who *is* life.

I am comforted that Peter and Jean-Paul are alive because God's eternal Spirit lives in them. Just as a seed planted in the ground withers and dies, producing new life, so is our hope when it comes to the resurrection of the dead. Our earthly bodies may die, but at the resurrection they are raised, imperishable. What a marvellous future there is in store for those who put their trust in our eternal God. As Corinthians 4:18 says: "So we fix our eyes not on what is seen, but on what is unseen, since what is seen is temporary, but what is unseen is eternal."

Reaping joy

Those early days of grief made me to want to hide under my duvet cover and go into hibernation mode. However, this desire was denied by my two demanding dogs, who needed their early morning walks. Then there were all the responsibilities of keeping a home together. The garden needed tending, the house had to be cleaned, bills were due to be paid and shopping had to be done.

On top of that, I needed to keep my part-time job. It was difficult to put on a brave face when I was broken inside, feeling disconnected from life and just going through the motions as I tried to keep everything together. I was incredibly thankful that my children supported me so well, helping out with practical tasks and just being there at the end of the phone to talk or meet up.

In all the difficulty of life and the toil of work, tears were never far away. It felt as if sorrow would never leave, as the weeks turned into months. There were days when I wanted to quit, but it was in those moments that I knew giving up was not an option, as I couldn't conceive of throwing in the towel in the middle of a fight. I was compelled to persevere. It was in the bleakest of times that I began to clearly see and know that God was still my rock. Through the storm of emotions I was being pushed into God and strengthened to stand on my own two feet.

Experience had taught me that my circumstances would not bury me in sinking sand, although there were days when it felt as if I were drowning in grief. It helped to know that even the bad days were part of the grieving process. My emotions were transient, but there was a stability beneath it all; a solid ground of resilience that would never give way. Jesus was my eternal anchor, keeping me moored to him. As Hebrews 10:39 says: "But we do not belong to those who shrink back and are destroyed, but to those who have faith and are saved."

Peter's parting caused me deep heartbreak. However, there is a promise in Psalm 126:5-6 that:

Those who sow with tears
will reap with songs of joy.
Those who go out weeping,
carrying seed to sow,
will return with songs of joy,
carrying sheaves with them.

Any hope of joy was buried beneath the all-encompassing weight of loss, yet the promise of joy was something positive for me to hold on to. God gives us his sure promise that "weeping may endure for a night, but joy comes in the morning" (Psalm 30:5). The psalmist describes this turnaround of tears as reaping a reward of joy, and my own experience has taught me that it is possible to live a fulfilling life after grief. The seeds of my tears will always produce a harvest, and in due season I will see it. The thought of better days ahead shone a glint of light, a hint of hope, into my circumstances, giving me the expectation that the night would one day be eclipsed with a bright morning.

Sorrow and suffering are never far from our lives, but we know that there will come a day when our tears are wiped away forever, when "there will be no more death or mourning or crying or pain, for the old order of things has passed away" (Revelation 21:4). This is the glorious hope for those who put their trust in our eternal God. In the meantime, grief will always give way to something good; to something joyful. No matter what happens, we will laugh again. And one day, we will rejoice.

Reflection

Your grief may feel all-consuming and never-ending right now. But just as we can be certain that the seasons will change from winter to spring, summer to autumn, so in the passing of time will your tears become less. In time, the hope of better days will rise up to greet you with new joy.

Prayer

Thank you, Father, that you see my tears as healthy and healing. As I cry, I am comforted by the thought that one day my joy will return. Amen.

Chapter Five

The Sparrow

Are not two sparrows sold for a penny?
Yet not one of them will fall to the ground
outside your Father's care.
(Matthew 10:29)

Travelling up to the Cotswolds in July 2021 with Tina and another friend, Jenny, provided a welcome break from life back home. My sister Liz and her husband Bryn kindly let us stay in the beautiful barn attached to their home. They live on a hilltop overlooking the rolling countryside, offering a perfectly tranquil setting to get away from it all and unwind. The blue skies rewarded us with glorious sunshine, so we spent a considerable portion of our time lounging about outside, enjoying the views and good company. It was the perfect tonic.

Light refreshments on the lawn were the order of the afternoon one particular day. Jenny had already headed outside, and as I joined her, she warned, "Oh, be careful of the bird!"

There on the ground was a young sparrow in obvious distress, its feathers puffed up and its little eyes squeezed shut. We deduced that the stunned bird had flown into the window, and there it lay on the ground. Several red kites were circling overhead, soaring on the wind current. I figured this little bird would be easy prey in its vulnerable state.

We prayed the little sparrow would be safe and restored back to life. We felt as if we were its guardians as we watched over it, protecting it from further harm.

Ten minutes passed and our little bird began to show positive signs. Its eyes opened and its head moved around as it began to engage with its surroundings. I was willing this injured bird to get better, and sure enough we were rewarded with the joy of seeing it fly up to the safety of a bush nearby. It was a glorious moment, and it thrilled our hearts that our little sparrow had survived. It was amazing that such a tiny thing could bring so much joy, but it completely brightened our day.

Still in shock

It was several hours later, as I reflected on the incident, that God's word came to me. It was an unfolding revelation of his love. He said: "You are like that little bird in shock. You have hit a hard place and you cannot move forward just yet. The world is carrying on as it does, but you're not. You are in recovery. Give yourself time to heal. Do not be afraid; you are worth more than many sparrows."

The trauma of losing Peter had brought my life to a crashing standstill. The shock had completely detached me from my world – launching me into one that was swirling, like a grain of sand shaken up in a snow globe. Everything had changed from that moment, as there was nothing I could do to bring Peter back. I was that fragile sparrow on the ground in need of rescuing.

A sparrow seems like an insignificant bird in the grand scheme of things, yet God notices when even one falls to the ground. Such is the knowledge of God that nothing escapes his attention. He is attentive to the minutest details of our lives. He sees and knows everything about us. As Matthew 10:30 says: "And even the very hairs of your head are all numbered." I had been knocked down, but my injury mattered to God. He was watching over me in the same way that Jenny, Tina and I had kept watch over our little bird. My Father's obligation was to keep me secure under his wing of protection.

The recovery process

I am normally quite a patient person, but the thought of my recovery taking time fuelled an impatience within me. I begrudged the idea of my life being on hold; it was an unwelcome interruption. But there had been a serious injury and there was no quick fix. Grief had wounded my very soul, affecting my mind, heart and emotions. Its wound was invisible, but it was real and deeply painful. Giving myself time to recover was unavoidable.

I knew that Peter was home, enjoying the rewards of God's eternal kingdom, but I had been left behind, damaged. My life didn't bounce back after the funeral. In fact, that was the time when the reality of my situation really began to sink in, and my zest for life vanished. It would take time to adjust to a new way of living that I hadn't chosen or wanted. However, in the devastation of loss, God stepped in and began a process of healing that was tailor-made for me. Our wise Creator knows us individually and has a purpose-built recovery plan for each of us.

Part of my recovery involved creating the space to grieve and offload my emotions. It mainly happened behind closed doors or outside in places that were devoid of people. I felt polarised from the rest of the world, which was oblivious to my plight.

I found it strange that the passing of a loved one could quickly become a taboo subject. I suppose it's because people don't know what to say, so they remain silent. It is often easier for grief to remain out of sight and mind, to sweep it under the carpet in the hope that one day the grieving person will resurface and fit back within the status quo.

Even among our church families, things that are said with the best intentions totally miss the mark. I think we are so umcomfortable seeing people in mourning that we try to remedy it by assuring them that their loved one is with the Lord, and of course this is true. But we're grieving because we love and miss them, not because they're in heaven. I haven't lost my faith because I'm grieving; the two elements co-exist. In fact, bereavement caused me to hold on tighter than ever to my faith.

I like the idea of grief being out in the open, expressed and understood. The Bible says that we should "mourn with those who mourn" (Romans 12:15). Perhaps the Western world could learn a thing or two from other cultures where families come together and mourn, bearing their hearts to one another. This seems like a much more wholesome approach to me. Whichever way you view bereavement, having someone come alongside you, offering you time to listen or giving you a reassuring hug and a hand of comfort, is a wonderful way to support a person on what can otherwise be a very lonely journey. I was so thankful that Tina looked out for me so well and made herself available to listen. I will never forget her acts of kind-heartedness and compassion. I think I would have sunk into despair without her support.

Even so, I never wanted to be in this position again. The pain of Peter's parting had reopened memories and scars of grief that extended back to losing Jean-Paul. I wondered how I would ever survive this pain, and it often felt as if the enemy were circling like the red kites, ready to swoop in for the kill. Yet God's word to me was: "Do not be afraid."

Any fear I felt at first had been drowned out by the shock and grief of a broken heart, but as the days passed, the fear of walking through the rest of my life alone confronted me. It loomed up, speaking irrational words into my mind in a bid to hold me captive. However, the fear of the unknown drove me further into my Father, and I discovered that his love was the perfect remedy to send those fears packing. The more I rested securely in his love, the less that fear was able to hang around. God really was my refuge, my hiding place.

Songs of comfort

For many months, grief was a place of captivity. My joy vanished and my heart lost its song, weighed down in a prison of sorrow. I could relate to Psalm 137, written at a time when God's people were held captive in Babylon, away from their homeland and unable to sing the songs of the Lord. The people wept and hung their harps on the poplars as they remembered Jerusalem, while their tormentors' demanded songs of joy.

I spent many a day remembering all the joy and fun Peter and I had shared. Those happy memories flooded my mind and made me long for that time when our home had been full of life. At this point my home was empty and so was my heart. To break the deafening silence and turmoil in my mind, I started listening to worship songs on Spotify. I often listened to Ian White, a vocal artist from the eighties who set psalms to music. I played them on repeat, both at home and in my car. The volume cranked up, these psalms would blast out the word of God, and it helped me so much to hear something positive. Little by little, the words soaked into my mind and spirit, and I would wake in the night with them repeating in my head. I became aware that God was communicating his love and singing songs of comfort, hope and life over me.

Zephaniah 3:17 says:

The Lord your God is with you,
The Mighty Warrior who saves.
He will take great delight in you;
in his love he will no longer rebuke you,
but will rejoice over you with singing.

This Scripture reminds me of a mother delighting in and singing over her child as she gives it nurture. She offers love and security as her child grows and embraces life. It paints a tender picture of our Father's love and his delight in reaching out to us.

Singing is such a powerful life force; it awakens and stirs my whole being. King David understood this and was no stranger to grief himself. Even when he was pushed back by his enemies and about to fall, his confession of hope was:

The Lord is my strength and my defence;
he has become my salvation.
(Psalm 118:14)

And:

By day, the Lord directs his love,
at night his song is with me –
a prayer to the God of my life.
(Psalm 42:8)

Listening to praise and worship has always been vitally important to me. It is a channel for prayer that allows me to express my love and thoughts to God, and God has guided my life through song many times. Meditative worship lifts my spirit to see into the heavenly realm and encounter the giver of all life.

In a similar way, the uplifting sound of birdsong can cheer the weary heart. I love to hear birds chirping away outside my bedroom window during the spring months. Have you noticed the way they sing in the dark before the light breaks in anticipation of a new day? In the valley of grief, song lifts the gloom and invites light into the shadow of loss.

I am sure our little sparrow found its chirpy song again once it had fully recovered. Listening to scriptural music became a vital source of restoration and revived my soul until my heart could find a new song to sing.

Around this time, God spoke a word that I didn't understand until months later. He said: "The psaltery is in you."

I was baffled. I knew the psaltery was an instrument, but why would it be in me? It wasn't until I started writing this chapter that I decided to google for more information. There, to my surprise, was a video of a man demonstrating the sound of the psaltery. He mimicked the sound of a fountain and various other everyday sounds with it, and I was moved to tears as I listened to its heavenly notes.

It suddenly became clear that the Holy Spirit was ministering the heavenly rhythm of the psaltery within me, gently bringing healing to my soul as I spent time listening to worship music. Wow! Heaven's sound waves. I began to see worship in a different light, noticing how anointed song and music connected to heaven's chorus could bring me into the very presence of God. No wonder people get healed when heaven touches earth through anointed singers and through musicians who are sensitive to the moving of the Holy Spirit. God was opening my spiritual eyes to a deeper understanding of his gentle musical ministry. He was soothing my grieving soul with the gentle sounds of heaven.

A broken vessel

Our little sparrow had escaped danger and found the safety of the bush. I, too, had "escaped like a bird from the fowler's snare" (Psalm 124:7). I ran to God's safety until I was hidden and cocooned in his loving embrace, and he faithfully shielded me from harm. There I could recover, as God set in motion his plan of healing for my broken heart. I woke every morning asking God to get me through the day. I was completely dependent on him. I found there was great liberation in the surrender, in the relinquishing of my life. I could not save myself, but I knew God would. I let go and let God do what he needed to do.

As Psalm 27:5 says:

For in the day of trouble
he will keep me safe in his dwelling;
he will hide me in the shelter of his sacred tent
and set me high upon a rock.

I often listened to the words of a worship song called "You Are My Hiding Place", based on Psalm 32:7, which says:

You are my hiding-place;
you will protect me from trouble
and surround me with songs of deliverance.

Who can comprehend the deep sorrow of a broken heart? Only those who have experienced it. Brokenness is something we don't discuss much in Christian circles. It's not a popular subject. After all, no one wants to end up down broken alley. It's the place to be avoided and should bear a signpost saying: "Do not enter." But David wasn't ashamed to talk about it. In Psalm 31:12 (NKJV), he writes:

I am forgotten like a dead man, out of mind;
I am like a broken vessel.

We would all rather be part of the victory parade for all to see. Yet the touching truth is:

The LORD is close to the broken-hearted
and saves those who are crushed in spirit.
(Psalm 34:18)

God never turns away the broken-hearted. Instead, he draws alongside us in our grief. To avoid pain and brokenness is to miss the divine appointment of God. To face pain head-on is to discover that he is already there, waiting to meet us. We can be broken by life's hurts, but pain can also allow God to shine the light of his glory into our despair.

I can relate to the story of the 300 pitchers carried by Gideon's army, which were smashed on the ground so the light of the torches could be seen (see Judges 7:16-20). You see, brokenness is a place of surrender, where the two states of being meet together. It's the place where we come to the end of self and God's life takes over. Surrender opens the way for God to do his will on the earth.

As 2 Corinthians 4:11 says:

For we who are alive are always being given over to death for Jesus' sake, so that his life may also be revealed in our mortal body.

We were made to reveal Christ; to display his light, love and salvation. He is the treasure we carry. As 2 Corinthians 4:7-9 says:

> *But we have this treasure in jars of clay to show that this all-surpassing power is from God and not from us. We are hard pressed on every side, but not crushed; perplexed, but not in despair; persecuted, but not abandoned; struck down, but not destroyed.*

It is in the pressing of grapes that wine is poured out. It is in the crushing of olives that oil is produced. It is in the hard-pressing and surrender of our lives that Christ's power is revealed.

This strange paradox of death bringing life and suffering bringing joy is centred on the cross, where Christ's sorrow, mingled with love, ran down into a broken, dying world. Like the sparrow on the ground, I was struck down but not destroyed. I was in a weakened and vulnerable state, but God's all-surpassing power was enough to fix me. A broken heart drenched with tears is a soft, pliable clay in our Maker's hands. He is the Potter, and he has created me to shine his light, not to hide it away under a pitcher. I would rather be a light for his glory in the form of a broken vessel than a perfect jar that hides his light away.

Yet it is not my brokenness that defines me, but the power of Christ to restore, heal and bring glory to his name. As I yielded my life to him, he bound up my wounds, as a loving Father would. He put me back together and made me whole. I knew that he would use my restored life to help others who were broken. I saw that my own strength was a hindrance, but my brokenness, my weakness, gave God an opportunity to reveal his much greater strength and power. It was at this point that I really understood God's words to Paul in 2 Corinthians 12:9 when he said: "My grace is sufficient for you, for my power is made perfect in weakness." He did not despise me; he embraced me. I was worth far more to him than many sparrows.

Reflection

Do you feel shipwrecked, as though you have been smashed against the rocks of life? If so, run into the arms of your loving Father. It will be his delight to restore you, to pour his healing balm into your life, to soothe every sore and affliction. You can trust God with the broken fragments of your life. He will make you into something even more beautiful than before, enabling you to bring comfort and change to others. You will become a living testimony to the power and love of Christ.

Prayer

Father, you are the light in my darkness, my song in the night, and I know that you delight in me. I am worth far more to you than many sparrows. I invite you into my pain and choose to trust you with it. You know me inside out. You know how to heal me and put me back together again. Thank you for your mercy, your heart of compassion and your lovingkindness in restoring my life. Make me a witness to the power of your love, so I can reach out to others who are hurting and bring comfort, as you have comforted me. May my life bring glory to your name. Amen.

Chapter Six

The Raven and the Dove

And my God will meet all your needs
according to the riches of his glory in Christ Jesus.
(Philippians 4:19)

The raven

I had been looking forward to visiting the Tower of London in August 2021 with great anticipation. My sister Liz had kindly arranged the trip, and it did not disappoint. Our beefeater guide greeted us with great charisma, and the tour he gave was filled with wonderful drama. His lively character ensured a captive audience as we listened to the grisly histories of those imprisoned in the tower, many of whom had met their premature deaths as a result.

Much to our collective excitement, a raven flew down and perched on the wall next to the beefeater during the tour. The bird was very vocal with its deep croaking, constantly demanding attention. The man was quick to calm any fears and explained that he was the raven master who took care of the birds and fed them. We watched with delight as the bird took food straight from his hand.

I later discovered something interesting about ravens in

God's word. In Luke 12:22-4, Jesus said to his disciples (bold type mine):

> *"Therefore I tell you, do not worry about your life, what you will eat; or about your body, what you will wear. For life is more than food, and the body more than clothes.* ***Consider the ravens****: they do not sow or reap, they have no storeroom or barn; yet God feeds them. And how much more valuable you are than birds!"*

This is such a liberating scripture for all of us, especially in the days we are living in, when life is becoming very tough. The cost of living is on the rise and wages are not keeping pace. But God says we are not to worry. We need to hear this over and over again until his words infuse our lives, and we know, with all confidence, that God's word is his bond.

Why worry?

Confronting the reality of widowhood while earning only a small wage, the words of Jesus become my lifeline. In Luke 12:25-26, he says: "Who of you by worrying can add a single hour to your life? Since you cannot do this very little thing, why do you worry about the rest?" Worry is rooted in our own well-being. It is an expression of fear, and it stops us receiving from God. I knew right then that I had to let go of any worry, and I would not even entertain it. I simply brought it to the cross.

God tells us to consider the ravens and their way of life. The lesson of the raven serves to remind us that our Father will meet all our needs. The Tower of London trip gave me a perfect example of this, with the raven feeding from the raven master's hand in front of my eyes. These birds do not store up food; they live day-to-day. I could relate to this lifestyle. Adjusting to being on my own certainly had its challenges, and it was a case of taking everything one day at a time. I couldn't think about anything beyond that.

As I pondered the simple life of these birds, it occurred to me that the smallness of their form spoke of how our faith should be: childlike. All we need to know is that our Father has promised to provide. There is no need to question him. I pictured myself as a child running to my heavenly Daddy, knowing I was secure in his arms and confident that he would meet my needs. It was liberating, and I found it easy to trust him.

My only desire was to seek after God. In Luke 12:31, Jesus says, "But seek his kingdom, and these things will be given to you as well", and in Matthew 7:7 he tells us to, "Ask and it will be given to you; seek and you will find; knock and the door will be opened to you."

With its deep croaking, the raven boldly asked its master for food. He knew the hand that fed him, he was close enough to take the food from his master's hand and he found what he was looking for. Likewise, as I rested in my Daddy's arms, I could ask him for everything I needed and he was happy to give it to me. Of course he wanted to provide for all my needs. This is his commitment to me.

The raven is also mentioned in Elijah's story (see 1 Kings 17). Elijah told King Ahab that the Lord was sending a drought across the land. God had instructed Elijah to leave and hide in the Kerith Ravine. There the prophet drank from a brook and was fed twice a day with bread and meat by ravens. He had no need to worry about his daily sustenance or to think about what would happen the next day. This was God's provision, and there is no lack in God's economy.

David was also very confident about this. In Psalm 23:1 we read, "The LORD is my shepherd, I lack nothing," and in Psalm 37:25 he says:

> *I was young and now I am old,*
> *yet I have never seen the righteous forsaken*
> *or their children begging bread.*

The dove

It was around this time that God started speaking to me about another bird: the dove. In Genesis 8:7, we hear that Noah "sent out a raven, and it kept flying back and forth until the water had dried up from the earth". Then Noah sent out a dove, and twice it returned to the ark to find rest. On its third flight it did not return, which signified that the waters had receded. This meant it was safe for Noah, his family and all the animals to leave the ark and find rest on dry ground.

The raven teaches us that God will meet all our earthly needs, while the dove – which represents the Holy Spirit's presence in our lives – leads us in God's ways and gives us rest. As Exodus 33:14 says: "My Presence [Spirit] will go with you, and I will give you rest."

The dove became the most meaningful part of my grief journey as God unveiled something very deep and intimate, revealing the incredible ministry of the Holy Spirit. I began to research doves, and to my utter amazement I found there was a species called the "mourning dove". These birds are known to vocalise a lot and were given the name because of their mournful call.

I pictured the Holy Spirit beckoning me to come closer. His voice spoke comfort into my grieving spirit. Like the mourning dove, he was grieving with me, wooing me back to himself with his love as I mourned the loss of my husband. It was at this point that I truly understood the words of Isaiah 38:14:

I cried like a swift or thrush,
I moaned like a mourning dove.
My eyes grew weak as I looked to the heavens.
I am being threatened; Lord come to my aid!

My tears flowed freely as I thought about the gentle and compassionate ministry of the Holy Spirit. He is love, joy, peace, forbearance, kindness, goodness, faithfulness, gentleness and self-control (see Galatians 5:22-23). This is the fruit of his presence, and his nature is evidenced in our lives as we yield to him. He is a wonderful Counsellor, who cares deeply for his hurting ones.

My relationship with God grew closer and deeper as he guided me through the valley. He spoke to me as his beloved one, like an echo of Solomon's words in Song of Songs 2:13-4 (NKJV):

Rise up, my love, my fair one,
And come away!

O my dove, in the clefts of the rock,
In the secret places *of the cliff,*
Let me see your face,
Let me hear your voice;

For your voice is *sweet,*
And your face is *lovely.*

In my secret place, hidden in Christ my rock, he has called me into a relationship of intimacy. His delight is in hearing my voice every day, and mine is in spending time with him face to face, not turning away. He has constantly affirmed that I am lovely to him, and that my voice is sweet. He is my mourning dove, awakening me from my brokenness and calling me out of hiding to flap my wings as I discover a newfound freedom.

Reflection

You can know God's provision even when there are food shortages. If God can feed Elijah with the help of ravens, he can feed you. Food supplies may be restricted, prices may rise and there may be famine in many parts of the world. But what will your response be if hunger comes knocking at your door? Will you trust in Jehovah Jireh, the God who provides? Or will you panic and worry? Staying close to the Father is the remedy for our problem of worry. Keep yourself hidden in Christ, your rock, who will meet all your needs.

Prayer

Jesus, help me to spend time with you, even in the busyness of the day. You are always waiting for me, calling me to draw close. I love you and thank you that you satisfy me with the fruits of your love so that I may, in turn, offer them to a love-starved world. Amen.

Chapter Seven

Royalty

But you are a chosen people, a royal priesthood, a holy nation, God's special possession, that you may declare the praises of him who called you out of darkness into his wonderful light.

(1 Peter 2:9)

As time went by, the Holy Spirit opened my eyes to see more of God's heavenly kingdom. He gave me pictures in my spirit to help me understand the truth and encourage my faith..

On one such occasion I listened to an online ministry, and at the end of his word the pastor started talking about crowns. As I listened intently, I suddenly saw a crown in my spirit. Many crowns are mentioned in the Bible in relation to the believer, but I believe the crown I saw was God's promise to me. It was a crown of beauty in place of ashes (see Isaiah 61:3).

A week later I tuned in to the same ministry and the pastor asked everyone to hold out their hands to receive something from God. As I stretched out my hands, I immediately received what looked like a sceptre. The Holy Spirit was reminding me that I belonged to a royal kingdom. Our lineage, our birthright, is that we carry God's kingly name everywhere we go. For Jesus "has made us to be a kingdom and priests to serve his God and Father" (Revelation 1:6).

There were a couple of occasions when I saw King Jesus standing by my side, wearing his crown. I knew he was encouraging me to be strong and confident. Bereavement and the wound of abandonment had caused an identity crisis within me. I felt as if my identity had been left behind with the parting of Peter. I had hit rock bottom and no longer knew what my purpose in life was. But the Holy Spirit was breathing new life into my spirit and building me up, reassuring me that I was a loved and highly favoured daughter of the King. The more time I spent with him, the more my identity became established in his stature, confident of my birthright.

As Isaiah 61:10 says:

For he has clothed me with garments of
salvation
and arrayed me in a robe of righteousness,
as a bridegroom adorns his head like a priest,
and as a bride adorns herself with her jewels.

The crown jewels

The crowning glory of the Tower of London was undoubtedly seeing the crown jewels. It was a special moment as I gazed with wonder at those precious stones of varied colours, crafted exquisitely and mounted into the gold crowns. It was mesmerising to see so many jewels all in one place. In Zechariah 9:16, God says that we are like jewels:

The LORD their God will save his people on that day
as a shepherd saves his flock.

They will sparkle in his land
like jewels in a crown.

God looks at us – diamonds in the rough, formed in the depths of the earth under great pressure – and sees the potential of a scintillating gem. We see our faults, our failings and our pain, but he sees a work in progress. He is the master jeweller who gently takes hold of our lives. Secure in his safe hands, he cleans and shapes us, knocking off our rough edges and smoothing out our imperfections. He simply asks us to yield to him as he gets to work.

The end result is infinitely worth it, as our lives change to reflect his brilliance. We are all different in shape and colour, each of us reflecting something distinct about the beauty of God. Together we shall be his crowning glory. As Isaiah 62:3 says:

You will be a crown of splendour in the LORD*'s hand,*
a royal diadem in the hand of your God.

We are Jesus' rare treasure – valuable and highly esteemed – and it is his great joy and delight to hold us in his hand for all to see.

Among the crowns at the Tower of London were several sceptres. The one that caught my attention was the Sovereign's Sceptre, topped with an enamel dove with opened wings perched on top of a cross. I felt awed and humbled as I looked at these two symbols together. This type of sceptre is held at a coronation to symbolise the monarch's pastoral care over their people and their sovereign role as Defender of the Faith. The dove represents the Holy Spirit, a reminder to the monarch that their authority comes from above.

It was at this point that I really understood why God had

given me the picture of the sceptre. It represented the power and authority I had been given as a member of God's royal family. This revelation gave me renewed strength and courage. The presence of the dove reminded me that the Holy Spirit is with me always, and it is in *his* authority, not my own, that I am able to live a life of victory in Christ. Whenever I feel as if I can't go on because my grief is so painful, I picture myself holding that sceptre and standing beside my King, who loves and cares for me.

The sceptre of authority

Thinking about this sceptre drew my attention to the book of Esther. Here we see a woman who eventually became queen as a result of her obedience. She prepared a banquet for the king and for her enemy, the wicked Haman, who had sprung a plot to have all the Jews slaughtered.

One of the ways Esther prepared herself to become queen was to bathe in oils. For six months she bathed in the oil of myrrh – the same oil used to anoint Jesus for burial. Myrrh represents our willingness to lay down our lives for the good of God's kingdom. Oil represents the Holy Spirit.

Esther purified herself so she could go before the King. Then she made the decision to come out of her place of safety for the sake of her people. When Esther approached the king, he held out his sceptre and she touched the tip of it, recognising his favour towards her. Her obedience and bravery led to the downfall of wicked Haman, and Esther became the voice of deliverance for her people, saving them from seemingly inevitable death.

As I reread the book of Esther, I saw how I had been living in a place of darkness for the previous six months, drowning in my tears. Unbeknown to me, this had been my place of surrender and obedience to the Holy Spirit. It had represented my tomb, my body having been bathed in myrrh as a sweet incense to God.

I knew I couldn't stay in this place of mourning forever. I needed to rise up from that place of death and embrace new life – the wonderful resurrection life we can walk in as we serve the King of kings. I held on to the fact that he had given me his sceptre of favour; his seal of approval to enter the royal courts of heaven and to decree the demise of enemy strongholds. As Hebrews 4:16 says: "Let us then approach God's throne of grace with confidence, so that we may receive mercy and find grace to help us in our time of need."

Jesus defeated Satan at the cross. He took back the keys of authority and handed them to his Church. Now all creation waits for the sons of God to be awakened to this truth, and to walk in that authority and become a voice for him. It became clear to me that I needed to make a stand or I would suffer at the hands of the devil, whose aim is always to steal, kill and destroy (see John 10:10).

However, many dangers were lurking as I walked through the minefield of grief. The enemy was constantly looking for a way to defeat me, whisper his lies and keep me downtrodden. I had to be alert to his accusations. I had to fight with the authority that had been given to me by God, which he had confirmed in the sceptre vision. As I spent time drawing closer to Jesus in worship and communion, he drew closer to me. It was only then that I truly knew I could resist the enemy and he would flee. God was teaching me afresh how to fight from a place of rest. Jesus said to me: "Stay close to me, for I am your shield of protection, your victory. No enemy can penetrate or stand against the sceptre of my authority and the sword of my mouth."

My Shepherd

The description on the sceptre used during William the Conqueror's coronation in 1066 read: "For by the sceptre uprisings in the kingdom are controlled and the rod gathers and confines those men that stray."

The sceptre is essentially a rod. During his time as a shepherd boy, King David would have known how to use the rod effectively as a tool to defend his sheep. It would have been used as a rod of protection. Psalm 23 speaks of God's care for us. He is our shepherd, whose rod and staff are used to comfort us.

I began to see that Jesus, my Shepherd, had gathered me, his injured sheep, into his pen, which was a confined enclosure. He was my gatekeeper keeping watch, and I was protected, comforted and given time to heal from my wounds. I knew that at the right time my Shepherd would lead me out into new pastures. In the meantime, he was teaching me how to fight, and how to rule and reign with him from a place of surrender and humility.

This picture of the shepherd using the rod of authority is one of gentle guiding. I was being taught how to use authority in the correct way. It was not the way the world would understand power and authority, which can be heavy-handed and demanding of people. Jesus' authority came from a place of service, respect for others and ultimately laying his life down for his flock (see John 10:14-15).

These wonderful truths helped to heal and restore my soul and mind. It was like God's anointing oil being poured on my head and imparting life. My Shepherd had prepared a table of abundant goodness that would meet all my needs: spiritual, physical, mental, emotional and financial. As his guest at the table, no robber could come near to steal from my life. The enemy could only stare at me from a distance (see Psalm 23:5).

I was protected in the sheep pen, being looked after by my Shepherd. With his help, I knew I could face this valley of the shadow of death without fear. I was confident that he would bring me safely through.

Reflection

Your Shepherd is dependable. He will never fail to come to your aid. He is kind, gentle and fiercely protective. Rest assured that you are safe in his keeping. His goodness and love will follow you throughout your life, and you will dwell in his house forever.

Prayer

Dear Lord, despite my difficult circumstances I can be at peace. I know that you are always watching out for me, ready to defend me whenever I feel threatened or unsafe. With you by my side I can walk confidently, knowing that you are my Shepherd and my King. Instruct me in your ways, Lord, and I will happily do all that you want me to do to bring glory to your name. Amen.

Chapter Eight

The Goodness of God

Praise the Lord.
Give thanks to the Lord, for he is good;
his love endures for ever.
(Psalm 106:1-2)

Having had six months to come to terms with my loss, September 2021 proved to be a month of increased God encounter. It was a pivotal time that began to tip the scales for God to move his hand of favour and restoration in my life.

Angels all around

At the beginning of the month I again listened to the online ministry I had been regularly following during the lockdown of 2020. The pastor was sharing about angels, and he claimed that they regularly turn up while he is ministering, often revealing their names. I was intrigued, wondering which angel might be with me. Completely unexpectedly, the name "Tobias" popped into my mind, catching me off guard.

I immediately checked on Wikipedia and discovered that the name "Tobias" means "God is good". I was so surprised that I jumped out of my chair, not knowing whether to laugh or cry!

Sometimes we forget that the angelic realm is all around us. I know there are people who see and discern things in the angelic realm, and I also believe that as the darkness in the earth increases, God will open our eyes to see his angel armies. If we could physically see the angels – God's messengers sent to minister and aid us in the work of his kingdom on earth – I'm sure we would be more emboldened to speak out about Jesus and less afraid of other people and the threats of the devil.

It was at this point that I suddenly recalled the time when my son Luke stayed with me so he could do some DIY jobs around the house a few weeks after the thanksgiving service for Peter's life. The rawness of grief had taken its toll and I blurted out to Luke the bitter words: "God has not been good to me!"

Heartache and pressure have a way of forcing the issues of life to the surface. The negative thoughts I had been having were blasted out of the water as I marvelled at God's goodness in sending Tobias to me. My doubts were soon replaced with remorse and conviction as I realised I had called his character into question. I asked God to forgive me. I decided I was not going to let bitterness take root in my life. Its poisoned arrow needed to be removed, and it was God's goodness that drove it out.

In times of crisis, the level of trust we have in God becomes evident. I initially blamed God, as the words that came out of my mouth revealed. We know that our words are powerful because Proverbs 18:21 says: "The tongue has the power of life and death." What we say can either destroy or preserve life.

Grief brought me to a low place. I not only mourned the passing of Peter, but a pathway of tears opened up over my own failings, my own sin. The apostle Paul said in Romans 2:4 (NKJV): "Do you despise the riches of His goodness, forbearance and longsuffering, not knowing that the goodness of God leads to repentance?"

I never saw Tobias, but I knew without a doubt that he was with me because hope began to rise in my heart. Hope renewed the expectation that my circumstances would eventually change. I began to see that there was still a purpose and a plan for my life, and this spark of hope gave me the strength I needed to carry on. Knowing Tobias was there confirmed the fact that I was not alone. I felt comforted and encouraged as I saw the hand of God working his goodness, even in my grief. In fact, every time I saw his goodness I would think of Tobias and it made me chuckle. I knew how David felt in Psalm 27:13-14 (NKJV) when he wrote:

> I would have lost heart, *unless I had believed*
> *That I would see the goodness of the* LORD
> *In the land of the living.*
>
> *Wait on the LORD;*
> *Be of good courage,*
> *And He shall strengthen your heart;*
> *Wait, I say, on the LORD!*

His goodness opened my eyes to a future I hadn't previously been able to imagine without Peter. I revelled in the fact that God had a plan for my life, as we see in Jeremiah 29:11-14:

> *"For I know the plans I have for you," declares the LORD, "plans to prosper you and not to harm you, plans to give you hope and a future. Then you will call on me and come and pray to me, and I will listen to you. You will seek me and find me when you seek me with all your heart. I will be found by you," declares the LORD, "and will bring you back from captivity."*

Dealing with disappointment

My disappointment following Peter's death had created a dissatisfaction within me that compelled me to seek God. My circumstances would not allow me to rest. I needed answers to the questions that grief had churned up in my mind, so I pursued him relentlessly. His answer came in the form of Romans 8:28: "And we know that in all things God works for the good of those who love him, who have been called according to his purpose."

Knowing that God works for my good in *all* things turned everything in the right direction. I realised this also included my failures, my disappointments and my broken dreams. I have always struggled with failure, and it was difficult to accept that the things for which I had been trusting and holding on to God's promises had all been crushed. The plans Peter and I had made and looked forward to would never be realised.

Added to that, I felt the bitter disappointment of not seeing him healed in this life. Peter and I had spent days, weeks and months praying together, reading the word and sharing scriptures about healing. And we knew that Jesus had already paid the price for our healing on the cross. As a result, Peter not being healed was a harsh reality to accept. However, not all things that happen are good, because we live in a world tainted by sin, inhabited by an enemy who wants to rob us of life. Let's face it, bad things happen to good people. We are not immune to adversity, but we do have control over our responses. And it is our responses that determine the outcome.

I quickly realised that God is not the giver of bad things. Even as human parents we would never want any harm to come to our children because we love them. We only want to do them good. Therefore, no matter how dire the situations we face may be, we can rest assured that something good will come out of them if we choose to rely on our heavenly Father. I came to a settled place of resting on this promise of God's goodness, knowing he is working for my benefit.

I now refuse to hold on to those situations where I once felt robbed. I have chosen to release those disappointments, knowing that God always has the victory, even in loss, because his is an eternal battle that has already been won. There is a silver-and-gold thread of his redemption and glory running through our lives. We don't always see the full picture, but he is handcrafting something beautiful in each of us.

"The Tapestry Poem" (author unknown, but popularised by Corrie Ten Boom) was sent to me on a condolence card prior to Peter's funeral. The words convey how God works in our lives:

My life is but a weaving
Between my God and me.
I cannot choose the colors
He weaveth steadily.

Oft' times He weaveth sorrow;
And I in foolish pride
Forget He sees the upper
And I the underside.

Not 'til the loom is silent,
And the shuttles cease to fly
Will God unroll the canvas
And reveal the reason why.

The dark threads are as needful
In the weaver's skilful hand

As the threads of gold and silver
In the pattern He has planned.

He knows, He loves, He cares;
Nothing this truth can dim.
He gives the very best to those
Who leave the choice to Him.

The tapestry of our lives will at times involve trial, but just as the colours of the weave stand out against the darker thread, so our joy is enhanced all the more. We are safe in his skilful hands. He is working his good purpose in our lives, even in times of great darkness. We may not see what he is doing or what he is preparing, but we can trust that it will be good. "We are God's handiwork, created in Christ Jesus to do good works, which God prepared in advance for us to do" (Ephesians 2:10).

The heavens opened

My daily walk time with the dogs is also my prayer time. On the morning of the 10th of September 2021 I left the house without a coat, not anticipating rain. Yet sure enough, the heavens opened as I approached the woods. My only option was to head for cover under a tall sycamore tree, snuggled up against the trunk with the dogs by my side. The rain was falling heavily with no sign of relenting, and it quickly seeped through the canopy, soaking the ground. The only place that remained dry was the tiny patch of ground where I was sheltering.

I offered up a prayer, asking God to stop the rain long enough for me to get home. However, it quickly dawned on me that the answer I sought was in the dry ground on which I was standing. Very often we miss the hand of God in the small things, not realising that answers to prayer can come in the simplest ways, and when we are least expecting them. It looked as if I was going to be there for a while, but I sensed it was an invitation for me to talk to God and an opportunity to give thanks. I gave thanks for Peter's life, and for my family, friends and home. I even thanked him for the rain and for the shelter of the tree.

As I did so my spirit began to lift, sensing God's pleasure and basking in his goodness. There was no need to rush away. It was an eternal connection, and time was of no consequence in that precious moment. In the six months leading up to that day I had been so full of sorrow that thankfulness was in short supply. But as I gazed up at these tall, majestic trees, admiring the beauty of creation, I felt so grateful. The tangible peace and calm of God's presence blanketed my soul and I knew that all was well. That kind of peace is beyond our earthly understanding and can be experienced even when we are in pain. Orchestrated by my Father, it was a special time, and one of many that will always stay with me.

Eventually, the rain eased to a light shower. I could see patches of blue sky above me and a glint of sunshine peeking through the clouds. I felt as if the clouds were shifting inside me as the sun broke into my soul. This was my cue to head for home, and I returned with a skip in my step. It was a wonderful way to start the day, and I was grateful to have been held up with God under the sycamore tree in the pouring rain. Something was shifting within me. Hope began to arise as I thanked him for his goodness.

Giving thanks

A few days later I awoke with thanksgiving on my lips. I had been praising God subconsciously during the night, drifting in and out of sleep but aware of his presence. It was a beautiful morning and I enjoyed this peaceful moment, feeling quietly contented. Things were changing, and my circumstances no longer felt like a huge threat. Rather than wanting to get out of my grief as quickly as possible, there was an acceptance and I embraced each day instead of despising it. My focus was shifting to God's goodness, giving him the opportunity to move. The more I gave thanks, the more the negative emotions lifted.

Despite experiencing great adversity, the apostle Paul also learned the lesson of being thankful in all things. He exhorts us to: "Rejoice always, pray continually, give thanks in all circumstances; for this is God's will for you in Christ Jesus" (1 Thessalonians 5:16-18). And in Philippians 4:4-7 he writes:

> *Rejoice in the Lord always. I will say it again: rejoice! ...Do not be anxious about anything, but in every situation, by prayer and petition, with thanksgiving, present your requests to God. And the peace of God which transcends all understanding, will guard your hearts and your minds in Christ Jesus.*

Paul reminds us to fill our thoughts with things that are pleasing to God. There is wisdom in his words and good reason to heed them. Thanksgiving was key for Paul in all the trials he faced, and there were many. He was beaten with rods, stoned, whipped and put in prison. Three times he was shipwrecked and adrift at sea for a night and a day. He even faced danger from his own people. The list goes on, until it is almost unbelievable that one man could face so much trouble and survive. He was more qualified than most to say that we should continually give thanks despite our circumstances.

It took me a little while to start rejoicing, but it eventually came when I saw and gave thanks for the goodness of God. It sprang up when I began to thank him in all things. If we all rejoiced and prayed throughout the day – giving thanks in every circumstance, whether good or bad – there would be no room for worry, fear or doubt. God's peace, which guards our hearts and minds, would leave no room for the enemy to sow negative seeds into our thoughts.

A garment of praise

As I continued to give thanks, I heard my Father tell me to put on the garment of praise. I knew all too well what it was like to walk around with a cloak of mourning on my back. The tears I had cried, and continued to cry, were necessary, but I knew there would come a time when they stopped ruling my life. In the meantime, I had to choose to put on praise. As Hebrews 13:15 says: "Through Jesus, therefore, let us continually offer to God a sacrifice of praise – the fruit of lips that openly profess his name."

It goes without saying that I didn't always want to praise him in the depths of my grief. It was an act of exercising my will over my feelings. But as I began to give thanks to God, I couldn't help but praise him. The two actions naturally go together. The Bible says that we enter his gates with thanksgiving and his courts with praise (see Psalm 100:4). It is God's order, and the best way to meet him is with our hearts open to receive.

I could see at this time that he was inviting me to come right into his courts, and to give him my primary attention and focus. I was also aware of the enemy, Satan, who wanted to keep me from praising God by keeping me weighed down in sorrow. I could see through his tactics and knew it was time to act, and I continued to offer up a sacrifice of praise. God dwells in our praises (see Psalm 22:3), and when we give him praise we invite his glory to come and fill us. This is the very purpose we were made for, and that's why our problems fade and disappear like vapour in his presence. Praise lifts us out of the lowliest places and brings us into the holiest place.

Praise is powerful when it comes from a genuine heart of love. I knew my praise was mighty; it was my warring stance – one that would cause any strongholds or stubborn walls of opposition to come tumbling down. I thought of Paul and Silas singing praises to God in prison. They were in chains, yet they knew he was with them. I'm sure they didn't know what was about to happen, but the prison doors miraculously collapsed and all the prisoners' chains were loosed. Their attention was on magnifying God, and in that place of freedom nothing could keep them chained. It is our praise that shifts atmospheres and situations.

As I rose up in my spirit and began to praise again, no negative thought or depression could invade my mind. No chain could bind me while I was caught up in the One who is worthy of all praise. God began to change my perspective as I kept my focus on him. As I thanked and praised him, and saw more and more of his goodness, a way began to open for God to move his mighty hand of deliverance in my life.

I had always thought of my "garment of mourning" as the traditional funeral garb, and even when I wasn't wearing black I felt sombre and stricken with grief. By contrast, I imagined the "garment of praise" to be brightly coloured; the kind of thing I might have worn to a party. As I donned this imaginary garment (by starting to give thanks to God) my mood completely changed – just as it might have if I'd switched my dark mourning clothes for something really glamorous, only more so. It made me believe that there really would come a time when my mourning would turn to dancing if I kept wearing that garment of praise, giving thanks to him every day.

Reflection
May you look around today and see the evidence of God's goodness in the beauty of his creation, the smile of a loved one or the help of a stranger. May you see God's goodness break through as you give him thanks from a heart of praise. You are opening the way for the King of glory to come and fill you with his blessings.

Prayer
Father, I thank you that you are always good to me. You protect me with your love, astound me with your wisdom and shower me with your grace. You are awesome in all of your ways, and I give you all the praise. Amen.

Chapter Nine

The Swallow

Even the sparrow has found a home,
and the swallow a nest for herself,
where she may have her young –
a place near your altar,
Lord Almighty, my King and my God.
(Psalms 84:3)

I am constantly amazed at the many ways in which God speaks. On the morning of the 27th of September 2021, I awoke with a word so clearly imprinted in my mind that it was shouting for my attention. The word was "Arundel". I had no association with it and didn't even know what it meant. It sounded like a name from an enchanted world, yet there was a familiarity about it. I have learned from experience that when God speaks a word like this, he is inviting me to pray and search it out.

I looked the name "Arundel" up on Google, and to my surprise found that it was the name of a town and a castle in West Sussex. In fact, it's in the county where Luke and my daughter-in-law Hannah live. I also discovered that the history of the name connects it to the old French word *arondelle*, meaning "swallow", and that these birds are depicted on the town's coat of arms.

I knew it was no coincidence that the swallow was being brought to my attention for a second time. Just a week earlier I had visited Exmouth with Tina. We were browsing in a clothes shop when she pointed to a patterned shirt covered with swallows. It grabbed my attention, and I knew I had to buy it. My spiritual senses were buzzing.

In *Easton's Bible Dictionary*, the Hebrew name for "swallow" is *deror*, meaning "bird of freedom". According to the dictionary, it is "distinguished for its swiftness of flight, its love of freedom, and the impossibility of retaining it in captivity". The swallow spends all of its time in the air, apart from when it is nesting, when it rests and when it has its young.

I sensed something was afoot. I was on a puzzle trail, and I had picked up the scent. I contacted Luke and Hannah to ask if they knew much about the town of Arundel. They informed me that they had visited the castle a year earlier and conveniently lived only thirty minutes away. I arranged to stay with them on the 10th of October, and Luke booked tickets for the castle on the 12th.

A couple of days before my trip I received a third confirmation from God. During a car journey that I take on a weekly basis, I stopped one day at the traffic lights and looked to my right. There, attached to a pole on an industrial estate was a swallow-shaped flag flying in the breeze. I smiled and thanked God for confirming his word. It was all about the swallows.

Interestingly, both the swallow and the sparrow are mentioned in Psalm 84:3. I had read it many times, but my focus had always been on the Valley of Baka. At this point, God highlighted the two birds in this familiar portion of scripture. God had lovingly spoken to me through the sparrow during my summer encounter with the injured bird. He had assured me that his care and nurture would restore my life. But as I read the verse afresh, my attention was drawn to the concept of the swallow finding a home near God's altar, where she could safely rear her young. The puzzle was falling into place with each new clue and I was curious to see where it would lead.

Countless thoughts stirred in my mind as I pondered why God was leading me to Arundel. Did he want me to pray around the town and the castle? Or was Arundel to be a new home for me? Losing Peter had left me feeling restless. There was a deep churning inside; an emotional sandstorm that wouldn't settle. I had no desire whatsoever to stay in my house any more, as I found the silence unsettling. I missed the happy days when we had been there together, as a family. I yearned to be at rest but could never find it.

Taking flight

The day finally arrived to travel to Luke and Hannah's. Seeing them brought me so much cheer. It was comforting just to be in their company, and it immediately made me feel more secure.

The following day we drove to Birling Gap on the coast. Having never been to this part of the country before, it felt refreshing to explore a new area. We walked along the coastal path up to a lighthouse. It was a beautiful October day and the scenery was stunning, yet the uncomfortable, lurking feeling of loss began to resurface, threatening to spoil any happiness I might have enjoyed. I so missed having Peter by my side. The emptiness reminded me that I was broken, and my heart was weighed down with sadness. I wished it would go away – I hated feeling like that – but there was no escape.

It was soon time for our visit to Arundel. The castle looked magnificent, rising up from its hill and towering over the town.

We walked around the grounds, admiring its beautiful gardens, before touring the inside of the castle. God whispered in my ear: "Remember the swallow. It nests near my altar." I looked up at this beautiful, imposing castle and imagined a swallow nesting high up under the turrets. I thought of God as a strong tower, an ever-present help in times of trouble (see Psalm 46:1). How I needed him to be my strength right then.

As the day progressed, loneliness and sadness hung over me like a black cloud, making me question why I was even there. I missed Peter so much it was overwhelming. All I wanted to do was weep, but I fought back the tears, not wanting to spoil the day. I felt like a hopelessly lost person out at sea, being tossed by the waves with nowhere to settle. My home should have been with Peter, but he was no longer with me. I longed for a new place to call home. How could I go through the rest of my life like this?

Darkness descends

The following day I travelled back to Bristol, but not for long. I had arranged to meet Tina in the afternoon so we could travel down to Exmouth together for a sleepover in her caravan. I loved the thought of not having to go home, as I wanted to be on the move all the time. I felt like the swallow that rarely comes in to land.

Travelling down to the coast should have provided a great escape. We enjoyed the sea air, our walks along the promenade and the freedom of the great open spaces, but inside I still felt trapped. I began to offload to Tina the feelings of loneliness and grief that were gripping me. The weight of emotional emptiness I felt was completely crushing. Would I ever be free?

Sadly our trip was a short one, and it was soon time to return home. My travels for the week were at an end. I arrived back at the house and sat down for a moment to gather my thoughts. I had been expecting something more and felt foolish to have pursued nothing but a wild goose chase. Deflated and surrounded by unbearable silence, I went to bed early. Sleep was the only relief I could find.

I awoke the following morning gripped by a deep darkness. I felt as if I were drowning in its intensity. Anger was building like a pressure cooker about to explode. I grabbed a book that had been lying on my bed and threw it across the room. The tears flowed yet again, but this time they were accompanied by an explosion of anger and a furious tirade. The grief was so painful, and with it came a whole load of disappointment and frustration. It felt like the deepest pit. I just wanted God to take me home so I could be with Peter. How could I continue with my life, feeling like this? I couldn't see a way forward. It was all-consuming.

Then, in the midst of my despair, my heavenly Father spoke: "Remember the swallow, which nests near my altar. When you are up against it, make your home in me."

His words struck me like a shaft of light piercing through, illuminating my mind and soul. Why hadn't I seen it before? it was so obvious that God had been calling me to his altar. The driving, unsettling pain of loss and the churning restlessness I had been feeling were drawn to the surface, like a boil ready to be lanced. I collapsed to the floor in a heap, releasing all the poison and trauma into God's outstretched hands.

I felt a burning sensation as God performed a deep healing within me. His peace flooded my whole being as I lay on the floor. I knew that he was delivering me from something that had been impacting my life for a long time, and it was his kindness and mercy that set me free. The puzzle pieces finally fell into place. I could see that my Father had given me the revelation of the swallow and orchestrated the journey to Arundel because grief had caused me to go into fight or flight mode.

The loss of Peter had changed the normality of my life, and everything had instantly become uncertain, sending me into a state of total restlessness. I didn't know where to go or where to land. It was at this moment that God worked his plan of deliverance through my wanderings, effectively exposing the darkness and freeing me from its grip. I constantly marvel at God's ways and his infinite wisdom. His healing plan was perfectly designed to bring me to his altar; my real home and place of safety.

Freedom

Once again, surrendering to God became my doorway to freedom. Like the swallow nesting at the altar of God, I finally found my rest. The swallow was never meant for captivity, and captivity was never meant for me! I was born to be free in Christ Jesus. The chains of abandonment, bitterness, trauma and anger could no longer hold me hostage.

I knew that Christ had fought for me, triumphing over those emotions on the cross. I was confident that Calvary had changed everything. Jesus died for me so I could walk out a life of victory, overcoming the deepest grief, the darkest depression, and every chain of bondage and sickness. Jesus has given every one of us this divine exchange. Where there is brokenness he brings healing, where there is captivity he brings freedom, where there is mourning he brings comfort and joy, and where there is despair he brings praise. Out of the ashes, he crowns our lives with his own beauty.

This newfound freedom opened my eyes to the importance of inner healing. In 3 John 1:2 (NKJV), we read: "Beloved, I pray that you may prosper in all things and be in health, just as your soul prospers." The prosperity of our souls is connected to our physical health. Our souls can be damaged by wounds that have lain dormant in our lives for many years, holding us back from experiencing all that Christ paid for us to have: complete fullness of life.

How many of God's people are suffering from a wounded soul, a valley of depression or the bitter tears of bereavement or trauma and never get healed? We can carry wounds from childhood or from traumatic experiences that give the devil a foothold to rob us of God's blessings. These wounds must be taken to the cross, where Jesus carried and overcame them with his shed blood, that we might be healed.

Abandonment and trauma were my piercing wounds, my hidden valley of loss. But that valley was finally being filled with firm, solid ground: Christ himself. That sinking depression, that bitter feeling of loss, was at last being healed. He was restoring the landscape of my heart to fit his plans for a greater harvest in my life. Where once I had experienced barrenness, the ground of my heart was tilled and sown with seeds of tears that would flourish and bear fruit in due season. After years of captivity, I was able to enjoy God's abundance.

Isaiah 40:4 says:

Every valley shall be raised up,
every mountain and hill made low;
the rough ground shall become level,
the rugged places a plain.

In the days that followed this healing experience, the intensity of those agitated feelings dissipated and I began to settle in my home without feeling the constant need to get away. My heart was beginning to mend, and I began to embrace life once again without that deep depression and sense of loss. Yes, there were still waves of grief that hit at random times, but it wasn't accompanied by the same driving pain of bitterness and anger. The more time I spent in God's presence, the less grief I felt.

I still cry on occasions when I miss Peter – when I remember the good times and the love we shared – but I began to see that God was unveiling a future for me to walk in. I knew that his plans were for my good; to prosper me and not to do me harm. As I looked back over the months that had passed, I could see how God had orchestrated his plan of healing for my life. He had led me to this very moment of surrender to bring wholeness. I was reminded afresh that his ways are marvellous, and I could finally say, as Paul did in Romans 11:33:

> *Oh, the depth of the riches of the wisdom and knowledge of God!*
> *How unsearchable his judgments,*
> *and his paths beyond tracing out!*

Reflection

May you know that God is fighting for you as you lie down and rest in his presence. He is your stronghold, your mighty deliverer, and you can trust him. The battle is not yours, but the Lord's. His goodness will bring you through, and you will rejoice in his victory throughout your life.

Prayer

Thank you, Lord, for your victory on the cross. I come to you and lay down all my hurts, pains and burdens at your altar of healing. I lay my life down and thank you that your blood has cleansed me, making me whiter than the snow. I want to rise up now and serve you in your kingdom, to bring glory to your name. Amen.

Here are some scriptures I found helpful that you can meditate on and pray through:

The Spirit of the Sovereign Lord is on me,
because the Lord has anointed me
to proclaim good news to the poor.
He has sent me to bind up the broken-hearted,
to proclaim freedom for the captives
and release from darkness for the prisoners,
to proclaim the year of the Lord's favour
and the day of vengeance of our God,
to comfort all who mourn,
and provide for those who grieve in Zion –
to bestow on them a crown of beauty
instead of ashes,
the oil of joy
instead of mourning,
and a garment of praise
instead of a spirit of despair.
(Isaiah 61:1-3)

Now the Lord is the Spirit, and where the Spirit of the Lord is, there is freedom.
(2 Corinthians 3:17)

And you will know the truth, and the truth will set you free.
(John 8:32)

Chapter Ten

Home

Surely your goodness and love will follow me
all the days of my life,
and I will dwell in the house of the Lord
for ever.
(Psalms 23:6)

Maybe it's a female thing, but it always amuses me how obsessed we are with storage boxes for the home. Have you noticed that some shops have whole sections devoted to them? Every time I visit Dunelm with Tina we seem to gravitate towards the storage section, contemplating the next box to buy and what to put in it.

Let's face it, boxes are really useful. If you're very organised, you might even have them labelled. My attic room is full of them, packed with things I can't quite bring myself to throw out because I might need them some day. I have so many boxes of books, photo albums, household items, children's toys and memorabilia. It's great to be able to store these things away – out of sight and mind – as long as I know exactly where they are if I ever need them.

Dependency

Humans love to keep everything in order and neatly contained because we have a driving need to be in control of our lives. Secular teaching reinforces this, continually showing us how to become independent. As children we are taught to stand on our own two feet, and as adults we have no other choice. The Christian life, however, is the complete opposite. Spiritual growth happens within a deepening dependency on God; knowing that in ourselves we can do nothing, but in Christ we can do all things.

I have spent much of my Christian life having to unlearn the things I was taught as a youngster – letting go of the reins of wrong thinking, and of trying to work things out for myself. Adam and Eve fell away from a life of depending on God because they desired the knowledge to do things their own way. That is how we end up trying to put God in the boxes we have made for him and inadvertently creating a powerless religion of containment and control as we strive to do his work in our own strength.

To depend on God is simply to trust and abide in him. It is effortless and restful, and it is fruit-bearing. Jesus confirms this in John 15:4: "Remain in me, as I also remain in you. No branch can bear fruit by itself; it must remain in the vine. Neither can you bear fruit unless you remain in me."

When Peter was alive, we did many things together. We both worked from home, so we each had our little routines around the house. Together we made a good team, and I was left floundering after his death, missing his support. But as more responsibility for the household was thrust on my shoulders, it pushed me to depend on God more than ever. The void Peter left will always be difficult for me to accept, and I am still adjusting to this new life on my own, but I have found that as I rest in and trust God, he is doing so much more for me than I could possibly have asked for or imagined (see Ephesians 3:20-21).

Overcoming fear

As a young Christian I loved the teachings I found in God's word and wanted to know how to live in a way that pleased him. My thirst for truth was insatiable. You may say that this was a commendable thing, but when grief ripped through my life the second time – smashing all my labelled boxes of learning – I had to come to God afresh on my knees, seeking him directly for answers.

It was in the devastating pain of bereavement that I discovered a cycle of defeat within my own life. As I mentioned in Chapter Nine, deep-rooted abandonment had led me to put up a wall of protection in an attempt to avoid getting hurt, but it was driven by fear. It had been with me a long time and had made itself a cleverly concealed home in what I thought was a part of my identity. When my grief shook me to the core, this wall of self-protection came down, completely exposing me to the fear. Ecclesiastes 3:3 says there is "a time to tear down and a time to build". A tearing down was needed in order to fix the root cause of my fear.

Love wins the day

Fear had infected my thinking, causing me to strive and leaving me unable to receive the full, abundant life God had promised me. Once my abandonment had been surrendered at the cross, my heart was unblocked and those springs of living water, that deep river of God's love, welled up, gushing over me and driving out the fear. God's love has always been with me, but it was free to flow out in greater measure. His amazing love cast all the fear out of my life, changing my very thinking. As it says in 1 John 4:18: "There is no fear in love. But perfect love drives out fear, because fear has to do with punishment. The one who fears is not made perfect in love." And 2 Timothy 1:7 (NKJV) says: "For God has not given us a spirit of fear, but of power and of love and of a sound mind."

My heavenly Father's love was the remedy for all my insecurity. I had been searching for it all my life without knowing it. In an ideal world, all children would receive the love and nurture of two devoted parents, but many do not. I had experienced a love deficit during my early years that was finally being filled with God's love. Love is the most excellent gift, and without it nothing is gained. As Paul was well aware, even if we gain all knowledge and understanding but do not have love, we are nothing (see 1 Corinthians 13:2). I had a good knowledge of God's word, but it needed to be grounded in his love. As 1 Corinthians 8:1 says: "Knowledge puffs up while love builds up."

The greatest human need is to be loved and accepted, but these values can only truly be found in Jesus. Paul's prayer for the saints (us) was that they would "know this love that surpasses knowledge – that [they] may be filled to the measure of all the fullness of God" (Ephesians 3:19).

Love is the transforming power that changes lives. It is God himself. His love is our protection, our place of rest. His love wins the day. As Paul writes in Romans 8:35-39 (NLT):

> *Can anything ever separate us from Christ's love? Does it mean he no longer loves us if we have trouble or calamity, or are persecuted, or hungry, or destitute, or in danger, or threatened with death? ...No, despite all these things, overwhelming victory is ours through Christ, who loved us. And*

> *I am convinced that nothing can ever separate us from God's love. Neither death nor life, neither angels nor demons, neither our fears for today nor our worries about tomorrow – not even the powers of hell can separate us from God's love. No power in the sky above or in the earth below – indeed, nothing in all creation will ever be able to separate us from the love of God that is revealed in Christ Jesus our Lord.*

It was God's love that burst through the walls and doors into that place of fear where the enemy had kept me hoodwinked. I invited God into the darkest rooms of my soul. I opened up the gates of my heart for my King to come in on a highway of his love and peace, and it was his delight to enter. From the basement to the attic, everything had to be moved out of the way. The rooms had to be swept clean and all the junk removed. My home was made empty so that it was fit for his fragrant presence, his light and the delights of his company to come and fill it. There is nowhere better than being at home with him.

My loving Father took me on a real adventure while my life was still in tatters. He took hold of my hand and said, "Follow me." When I had nothing to give except a broken life, he said, "That's all I need. Now I will show you what I can do." The heavenly encounters and the places he took me to were all part of his divine set-up. All he asked of me was to trust in and surrender to him.

A heavenly campfire

When I think back to the adventures of my youth, I loved going camping with friends. I enjoyed the freedom of the great outdoors, the camaraderie and sitting under a starlit sky, singing songs around the campfire. King David was camped out in the wilderness with his band of soldiers. Exiled from home, and at his lowest point in life, I can easily imagine him sitting down and singing this psalm:

I will extol the LORD at all times;
his praise will always be on my lips.
I will glory in the LORD;
let the afflicted hear and rejoice.
Glorify the LORD with me:
let us exalt his name together.

I sought the LORD, and he answered me;
he delivered me from all my fears.
Those who look to him are radiant;
their faces are never covered with shame.

This poor man called, and the LORD heard him;
he saved him out of all his troubles.
The angel of the LORD encamps around those who fear him,
and he delivers them.

Taste and see that the LORD is good;
blessed is the one who takes refuge in him.
Fear the LORD, you his holy people,
for those who fear him lack nothing.

The lions may grow weak and hungry,
but those who seek the LORD lack no good thing.
(Psalm 34:1-10)

This psalm speaks into my journey and reminds me of being camped around a fire: a place to warm up, rest, recover and regain strength. In the valley of grief, when I was torn from my happy life with my husband, God pitched his tent in my heart. In sorrow I sought the Lord, exalting his name as I played my worship songs. The Lord sent Tobias the angel, who encamped around me and showed me God's goodness. He protected me and delivered me from fear as I gazed into the campfire of his presence.

It's a well-known fact that no ferocious beast lurking in the darkness will ever venture near the fire, and the heat also burned up all the stubble, dross and shame of past failures and disappointments. His love burned in my heart as I gazed on his beauty and radiated his likeness. In God's camp there is never any lack, and he has met all my needs abundantly.

Jesus has pitched his dwelling place in you, and the more time you spend in the warmth, light and fire of his presence, the more you will reflect his glory and walk in his ways. His love is a blazing fire – a pure flame – and he wants to burn brightly in you.

Inheritance

The journey I took to find my true home turned my attention to two characters in the Bible: Naomi, and her daughter-in-law Ruth. These two women walked through intense grief to eventually find blessing and restoration in God's house. I could totally relate to them, and their story gave me hope.

Naomi experienced multiple layers of grief. She lost her husband and two sons (one of whom was Ruth's husband). Can you imagine the sorrow anyone would feel at losing three loved ones? I understand why she wanted to be called "Mara" ("bitter") and questioned why God had brought such misfortune into her life. With her hands completely empty, Naomi prepared to return home to her place of birth and inheritance: her father's home in Bethlehem (which means "house of bread"). She had heard that the Lord was providing food for his people in the land of Judah (which means "praise").

Naomi discovered a relative on her husband's side whose name was Boaz (which means "in him is strength"). This was her awakened hope as she realised he was a "kinsman redeemer". This meant he was obliged to take responsibility for her and for Ruth; that he would have to rescue them out of their dire situation. We see Naomi's life go from full at the start of her journey to empty in her time of grief to full again after her (and Ruth's) encounter with Boaz. Her life was renewed and she became a grandmother. Her bitterness turned to joy, and she was sustained in her old age.

Like Naomi, I know that my home is in my Father's house. I am safe and provided for, and he is my praise. He is my redeemer, my living hope. He will save and restore all that has been lost.

And we shouldn't forget Ruth in the story. Recently bereaved, she chose to leave her homeland to start a new life with Naomi. She clung to her mother-in-law, declaring "your God [will be] my God" (Ruth 1:16). We can see God's redemptive plan unfolding as she begins to glean the sheaves in Boaz's fields and takes refuge under God's wings (Ruth 2:12).

Ruth obeyed Naomi when she encouraged her to go to the threshing floor at night and lie down at Boaz's feet while he was sleeping. Boaz awoke to find her there and knew what his obligation was to her as kinsman redeemer. He was obliged to marry her. One day Jesus, our Redeemer, will return for his bride (the Church), and take her home. Until then, I will lie at his feet, at his altar, just as Ruth did with Boaz. He is my place of surrender. It is in dying to myself that he gives me new life. Luke 9:23 says: "Whoever wants to be my disciple must deny themselves and take up their cross daily and follow me." This is resurrection life!

Arising from the threshing floor, Ruth stepped into a new, hope-filled future and a glorious inheritance. She married and gave birth to a son, who turned out to be the grandfather of King David. Having come from a place of great sorrow, she reaped great joy.

The story of Ruth reminds me of Song of Solomon 8:5, when he asks: "Who is this coming up from the wilderness leaning on her beloved?" It is from this place of intimacy with God, of abiding and nesting in him, that the birthing comes – just as the swallow nests near the altar to have her young. We were made to birth the plans of God. His desire is always to bring multiplication, which means that whatever God blesses us with is to be shared for the good of others. He wants to see increase in all that we do in order to bring praise and glory to his name. He is the God of abundance!

God turned Ruth's devastating situation around to bring great blessing. It encouraged me to know that he would also work out his redemptive plan in my life. Although I had suffered loss, I was comforted to know that God would redeem my sorrow. This was his loving heart toward me. Nothing had gone unnoticed. Nothing was ever wasted when I chose to trust, and I saw God's loving hand protecting and restoring my life first-hand. He has been so good to me. I see now that I am my Father's inheritance. I belong to him, having been purchased by the blood of Christ, and he belongs to me. This is the glorious hope to which he has called his Church (see Ephesians 1:18).

In Christ we have obtained an inheritance that cannot perish. It is our eternal home, kept in heaven for us. It is the

Christian's final destination. It is what enables us to keep going. "For our light and momentary troubles are achieving for us an eternal glory that far outweighs them all" (2 Corinthians 4:17).

Reflection

Your "home" should be a beautiful sanctuary; a familiar place to unwind and recharge your batteries. Your heavenly Father is inviting you to make yourself at home in him. It is his great delight for you to come and spend time in his presence. He will shoulder your burdens, delight in your love and encourage you to face each new day with joy. His home is permanent, and it is the happiest place to live.

Prayer

Father, I declare that I am at the threshing floor, lying at the feet of Jesus. When the time is right, I know you will get up and act on my behalf to make everything right. This is your obligation to me, your redeeming love, and I thank you for it. Amen.

Chapter Eleven

The Joy of a Friend

A friend loves at all times.
(Proverbs 17:17)

Friendship is one of the sweetest things in life. It's like tasting your favourite cake or enjoying the best flavour of ice cream. Tina brought delight into my world while I was in the mire of grief. She made me feel as if everything would be all right when I was falling apart at the seams. My faithful friend continually reached out, like a mother hen spreading her wing over me. She would call me night and day to make sure that I was OK. I knew I could rely on her when I was at my lowest ebb. She was a safe haven to which I could run at any time.

Our friendship was forged at infant school, and we vividly remember pretending to be birds in the playground. Tina was always the mummy bird, taking the lead, and nothing has changed since then. We both find it amusing that I have written a book about grief in the context of various birds. That well-known saying "birds of a feather flock together" has certainly been true for us.

When Peter was alive we often met up with our besties, Tina and her husband Steve. We would go for a coffee and walk around Bristol's docks. Over the years, our families holidayed together. Our friendship was deep-rooted and joyously celebrated. Therefore, losing Peter was a bitter blow for all of us. It was the end of something special. I had lost my best friend, but so had Tina and Steve. Somehow, the shock and deep sadness brought us closer together, reinforcing our deep bond. We are family, and it will always be that way.

The dogs became a drag

Still, life without Peter was anything but normal. The enormity of suddenly having to take care of the house as well as Pearl and Dime felt like a mountain to climb while I was still grieving. Peter had been the dogs' primary carer, walking them most mornings while I did the afternoons. After he died, I reluctantly had to take full responsibility. The dogs became my morning alarm clock. They were a source of irritation, their incessant whining driving me almost to despair. Sadly, they bore the brunt of my angry words while I was coming to terms with my grief.

Seeing this struggle, my dear friend Tina stepped in and suggested we walk our dogs together. This proved to be a great solution. We would meet up a couple of mornings a week, armed with flasks and equipped for every eventuality. Come rain or shine we would walk through the park, chatting and putting the world to rights.

Our favourite park had a community garden, offering a peaceful place to sit and eat. We visited it at the end of each walk, and it became our happy place. School children would visit to learn about different plants and how to grow vegetables. Young families would congregate. There was a safe play area for the children, where parents could watch while they chatted with their friends. It was an oasis of peace and well-being. Tina and I loved being outdoors. It was a welcome source of refreshment that set us up for the rest of the day. The dogs were happy and so were we. It was win-win all the way!

Walking my dogs has since become a delight, and I always look forward to meeting up with Tina and having some special time together over a coffee in the park. I am so thankful that the dogs forced me to get up in the mornings and face life. They are also great company at home, giving me comfort, love and their undivided attention. I wouldn't be without them.

A true friendship

Tina has been my greatest support and encourager throughout; a listening ear I could trust and confide in. When I reflect back on those early days of grief, I really don't know how I would have survived without her love and care. Having experienced the loss of loved ones herself, she was able to relate and understand the pain that sorrow brings. Over the years we have both been there for each other. We have walked life together. And as a result, our friendship is based on transparency rather than pretence.

God knew I needed a friend to talk to and share my life with. As humans we are created to relate and not to be alone. Yet sadly there are many who are lost in loneliness, hidden behind closed doors and disconnected from society. Dare I say it? Even in our churches there are people who are hurting, who feel like failures, who are broken inside. Where is the transparency among the people of God? Why do we so often pretend that everything is all right, when deep down we are in pain and in need of healing?

It saddens me to think that people are suffering in silence without having anyone there to meet the basic requirement for human contact. We all need to be loved and cherished. Bereavement is a lonely road, but having the support of someone who will walk by your side, and who is willing to listen and encourage you, is invaluable. Just knowing there are people who will be there can make all the difference.

Throughout 2021, Tina and I went on lots of little adventures. She and Steve were looking to move house, so we searched far and wide for a potential new home for them. It was a welcome distraction that got me out of the house, and her company was just what I needed, as she talked to me about her dream of owning a new home. We shared many laughs and joyous occasions as we scouted around for the next property to view. It kept my spirits up when I could easily have plummeted into a downward spiral.

Tina's strong mothering instinct often took over when I felt as if I didn't want to talk. She would cluck away about this, that and the other, and I would listen, occasionally nodding my head. Tina could talk the hind legs off a donkey. We can laugh about that because we know each other so well and appreciate each other's attributes. A faithful friend is someone you can be yourself with and feel accepted. We have been there for each other through all the highs and lows of life.

I am so thankful for all my friends. It is rare thing to have had a handful of friends since childhood who are all still in regular contact today. These are the same friends I climbed mountains with during my teenage years, and they have provided support, love and encouragement through the decades. I constantly marvel at the strength and power of real friendship. Proverbs 27:9 (TPT) says: "Sweet friendships refresh the soul and awaken our hearts with joy, for good friends are like the anointing oil that yields the fragrant incense of God's presence."

Feeling the joy

I had sweet friendships, so why was I not feeling the joy? I had been mourning Peter's passing for months by this point and had expected my joy to return. There were pockets of happiness, but then I would feel flat again.

I confided in Tina, who often came out with one-liners that dripped with the honey of wisdom. Her words to me were: "You have to *choose* joy." Those words began to unravel something as I thought about joy as a source of strength (see Nehemiah 8:10).

Tina has been like an oak tree of strength for many people, her arms spread out wide to offer a place of shelter and comfort. I knew I could lean in to her when I felt weak. Her strength has come from fighting her own life battles, and I have seen her grow through them. She has had to pick herself up and dust herself off countless times. She often says: "You have to be a radiator and not a drain," meaning that we should be people who "radiate" warmth and light as opposed to absorbing other people's light. She was so right and has always been that light of encouragement in my darkest moments.

As I pondered her pearls of wisdom, God whispered to me: "Tina is my joy to you. She has walked with you throughout your grief."

These words struck me deeply, causing a veil to lift from my mind. I realised she was the fragrant anointing oil of God's presence, awakening my heart to joy. Whenever I struggled she was there, shining her light of positivity, affirming and willing me onwards and upwards. How had I not seen it before? My precious friend, God's gift to me, had been my joy while I was in the deepest valley of grief. I thought of all the times we had laughed since Peter's death. She really had cheered me up.

With gratitude in my heart, I began to thank God for my dear friend. Joy had been there all along, but it had been hidden by my grief to the point where I hadn't recognised it. But my heart was finally awakened to joy through Tina. It was an empowering moment of realisation.

For the first time since my bereavement, I chose to listen to a song called "Catch the Wind". I had often played this song when Peter was alive. It had always been a favourite of mine, and it gave me goosebumps as I felt the liberating power of God when I listened to it. I played it loudly, belting out the words with every fibre in my being. The joy kept coming and coming. It was truly glorious!

Pain has a purpose

Friendship is God-given, and Jesus is the perfect example of a true friend. He chose us to be his friends and to share in the joy of that friendship. As he said to his disciples: "I have called you friends, for everything that I learned from my Father I have made known to you" (John 15:15).

His heart – and his joy – was to share the secrets of God's kingdom with his friends, so they too could partake of it. Friendship with Jesus is about being close to him; communicating well and sharing openly. When I think about my friendship with Tina, I see all the godly qualities Jesus requires in my relationship with him. He shared the greatest example of friendship when he said: "Greater love has no one than this: to lay down one's life for one's friends" (John 15:13), and that's exactly what he did.

Jesus had you and me in mind when he went to the cross. There was purpose in Jesus' pain. He endured the cross because he could see the reward waiting for him. That reward was us. The joy set before him was to open a way for his friends to enter his eternal home. That joy was worth all the pain. What love! It reveals the tender heart of Jesus towards his friends.

I thought about the pain a mother goes through in bringing a child into the world. The joy of seeing her newborn baby overrides all the pain she has to endure. The idea that pain has a purpose gave me great hope. It shifted my focus to the reward that would eventually result from it: eternal life with my Saviour. As Psalm 16:11 says:

> *You make known to me the path of life;*
> *you will fill me with joy in your presence,*
> *with eternal pleasures at your right hand.*

I remembered the heavenly encounter up in the fields when I had seen Peter and felt his embrace. It was his joy that I felt, but it was also the Father's joy. At the time my heart was full of pain and sorrow, having just lost my best friend. But as I write this chapter, more than a year down the road, I remember Peter's joy more than I remember my pain. I know that he is with Jesus, cheering me on from the finish line. I can almost hear him saying: "Keep your eyes on the reward!"

We are his friends

Fixing our eyes on Jesus is our ultimate joy. He has paved the way through all the difficulty and pain. He is not just on the finish line; he is also walking with us, hand in hand, through life. Because Jesus endured, we can also endure. James 1:2-4 says: "Consider it pure joy, my brothers and sisters, whenever you face trials of many kinds, because you know that the testing of your faith produces perseverance. Let perseverance finish its work so that you may be mature and complete, not lacking anything."

Our trials will always produce something positive. They have a divine purpose to develop godly character and to achieve eternal glory. As 2 Corinthians 4:17 says: "For our light and momentary troubles are achieving for us an eternal glory that far outweighs them all."

Jesus shared his life with his friends on the earth. They walked, talked and sat down together, savouring the joy of sweet fellowship. I could hear the words of Jesus as I thought of the many times I had spent with Tina at the park. He said:

> *I invited you to come and meet me in the park with Tina. I have been with you and walked with you. I sat down with you at the table in the community garden. This has been our place of sweet communion as you talked with Tina over a coffee, a pain au chocolat, or sometimes a bacon butty or a sausage bap. This is the place you both love to come to, where you want to linger. It is a slice of heaven; a place of rest and refreshment. This is my Father's house, and it is my joy when you come to my table to share my food and enjoy my company. You are my friends and I love you.*

Reflection

May you be blessed and refreshed by a true friend. May your joy bubble up and spill out for others to see. You have the power to change the atmosphere around you and brighten someone's day. You are God's shining light, ready to be put on display.

Prayer

Father, I thank you for the joy of good friends. I do not take them for granted, but treasure them for their love, strength, encouragement and a whole lot of laughs. They are precious, and I recognise them as your gift to me. Jesus, you showed me true friendship when you willingly laid down your life so we could be friends forever. Thank you. Amen.

Chapter Twelve

Mount Hermon

I will remember you
from the land of the Jordan,
the heights of Hermon.
(Psalm 42:6)

The presence of God was palpable as I drew near to him in worship one particular morning in November 2021. Expectancy hung in the air, and then I saw him: my Jesus in the form of a stag, bounding along a mountaintop. He appeared magnificent and exultant. I could see that he was triumphing over all that was happening on the earth; dancing with immense joy and freedom.

As I gazed up at him, and he looked down towards me, he said: "Come up here. You know this place. Come and meet with me."

I joined him on the heights, my heart captivated. I was infused with joy and exhilaration as I followed in his footsteps. Total freedom reigned in that place. The world below, with all its troubles, was unable to touch it. This was God's heavenly realm, where my beloved One wanted me to come and spend time with him.

As I marvelled in the moment, the scene changed. I was still on the mountain, but a little below the summit. Then I saw Jesus in human form, transcendent in his glory. I glimpsed his shining white robe, pure and radiant. It was a tangible, holy moment, and I longed to stay.

Then Jesus whispered to me: "Mount Hermon."

I was surprised by this, and it shook me out of my God encounter. I wondered why he had mentioned Mount Hermon. I immediately looked online and discovered that Mount Hermon is the tallest mountain in the most northerly part of Israel, in the Golan heights. It sits in the snow-capped mountain range that straddles the borders of Syria and Lebanon, and the River Jordan originates in its peaks. Its waters run south, into the sea of Galilee, then down to the lowest point on earth: the Dead Sea.

It thrilled my heart to discover that Israel has snowy mountains. I have always loved snow; it brings out the child in me and reminds me of purity. As Isaiah 1:18 says:

> *Though your sins are like scarlet,*
> *they shall be as white as snow.*

In Hebrew, the name "Mount Hermon" comes from the Semitic root *hrm*, meaning "taboo" or "consecrated". In Arabic, it means "sacred". In biblical times it was known by the Sidonians as *sirion*, meaning "breastplate", in reference to the mountains' rounded, snow-capped crests, which gleam in the sunlight.

This last description reflects how I saw Jesus in his pure radiance, like the gleaming snow. It prompted me to look up the account of the transfiguration, when Jesus took Peter, James and John up to a high mountain. As Matthew 17:2 tells us:

"There he was transfigured before them. His face shone like the sun, and his clothes became as white as the light."

Could Mount Hermon be where the transfiguration took place? The highest mountain in Israel would have been a fitting place for Jesus to be seen in all his glory.

Transition

Although the exact location is not specified in the Bible, it is interesting to note that Jesus was with his disciples in Caesarea Philippi prior to the event – north of Israel in the Golan Heights, and therefore close to Mount Hermon. It was here that Jesus began to explain to the disciples that he would suffer and be put to death in Jerusalem.

For three years Jesus had taught and performed miracles in their presence. Here they were being prepared for a time of transition, for a future when he would not physically be with them. In Jerusalem, Jesus told them: "You are filled with grief because I have said these things. But very truly I tell you, it is for your good that I am going away. Unless I go away, the Advocate will not come to you; but if I go, I will send him to you" (John 16:6-7).

He reminds them of this later in the same chapter: "Very truly I tell you, you will weep and mourn while the world rejoices. You will grieve, but your grief will turn to joy" (John 16:20). It must have felt like a crushing blow to the disciples' hopes and dreams of Jesus restoring the kingdom of God on earth when they saw him suffer the cruel death of crucifixion. Indeed, it was time to grieve in what was to be their darkest hour, but it was also a time of transition into a new era.

Similarly, my own grief was a place of transition; a confined space with seemingly no door to act as an escape route. It was a place of shadow and vulnerability, a road of unfamiliarity. It felt like I was in an aeroplane's holding pattern, unable to land. Transitions are painful places of testing and trial, but in them our faith is made strong and we mature.

Transformation

The glimpse of Jesus' shining robe that I had seen on Mount Hermon and the biblical account of the transfiguration began to speak to me of how we are being changed, as believers, as we go from glory to glory. In my confinement I had waited for God, and I had met with him. The more time I spent with him, the more I became like him. I could almost feel his character rubbing off on me. I could see that this place of transition was an opportunity for God to show his transforming power and glory as my grief was eventually transfigured into joy!

This was also true for the disciples when, after Jesus' resurrection, he appeared to them in Jerusalem and instructed them to wait for the gift: the Holy Spirit. The disciples were all gathered together in the upper room. This was a pivotal moment when the Holy Spirit came and filled them with his power and transformed their lives. Their grief had turned to joy, just as Jesus had told them it would.

As 2 Corinthians 3:17-18 says: "Now the Lord is the Spirit, and where the Spirit of the Lord is, there is freedom. And we all, who with unveiled faces contemplate the Lord's glory, are being transformed into his image with ever-increasing glory, which comes from the Lord, who is the Spirit."

Flying free, like eagles

My Mount Hermon encounter gave me an overwhelming sense of freedom. In the Valley of Baka I had waited in surrender while the Holy Spirit renewed my strength and carried me upward through my difficulties. And from that deep valley he had taken me to the highest place: the mountaintop. God had been true to his full circle word at the beginning of my journey, when he said that I would spiral up out of the valley. It was at this point that I fully understood what it meant.

Like the eagles who fly into the storm (yes, another bird God used to speak to me!) and let the wind push them up higher, so we must allow the Holy Spirit to lift us above our storms. We were made to fly; to catch the wind of God's Spirit, leaving our earthly problems behind. Eagles soar effortlessly on the thermals and can see for miles from their high vantage points with their sharp vision. In the same vein, we can face any mountain or valley of trouble with ease when we cooperate with the Holy Spirit. As Isaiah 40:31 says:

> *But those who hope in the* L*ORD*
>   *will renew their strength.*
> *They will soar on wings like eagles;*
>   *they will run and not grow weary,*
>   *they will walk and not be faint.*

When I was with Jesus looking down from the mountain, everything beneath me looked tiny. This was how God wanted me to view my difficulties: from his perspective. I knew I had to see my circumstances through my spiritual eyes if I wanted to live in this place of freedom, and not allow myself to be swayed by what I was seeing in the natural. As Colossians 3:1-3 says:

> *Since, then, you have been raised with Christ,*
> *set your hearts on things above, where Christ is,*
> *seated at the right hand of God. Set your minds on*
> *things above, not on earthly things. For you died,*
> *and your life is now hidden with Christ in God.*

It was from this place, way up high, that I could see and know victory, and I knew that God wanted me to be seated with him in this heavenly realm (see Ephesians 2:6). With Christ in me and I in him, there was no power that could overcome me because he had already won every battle over Satan on the cross. From this position, as a citizen of the kingdom, I could represent my King on earth with all authority, declaring, "your kingdom come, your will be done, on earth as it is in heaven", as Jesus taught us in Matthew 6:10.

The river of life

I was fascinated to discover in the course of my research that the River Jordan began its journey at Mount Hermon. My vision of the mountain painted a picture in my mind of God in his holy dwelling, with the Jordan as the river of life flowing out from his throne in Revelation 22:1-2. Similarly, in Ezekiel 47:1-12 we find a description of the river flowing out from the temple of God. It is a vision of Jesus, who has come to dwell with us. We are his living temple, and the river of his presence flows out from our lives, causing the barren places in other people's lives to become fruitful. I knew that if I got into the river and went with the flow, the Holy Spirit would bring healing to the deepest places of despair, pain and sorrow in my life. Even dead things come back to life in his presence. When we let go and let the Holy Spirit lead, we see his life everywhere.

His never-ending stream brings refreshment and gladness, as we taste and see that he is good. John 7:38 tells us that rivers of living water will flow out from those who believe in him and have received his eternal life. This is a picture of the Holy Spirit filling us so that we can overspill the good news of Christ's love to the hurting and broken. We are his living examples; witnesses to the abundant life and power of God. May we be carried by his river to bring salvation to a dying world.

Freedom for all

The day after I received the mountaintop vision, I walked the dogs up the well-trodden path to the fields, listening to worship music on my headphones. My heart was deeply stirred, and I encountered the Lord in a vision for the second time that week.

I saw Jesus standing before me. He pulled his outer cloak aside, and I embraced him, resting my head on his chest. I could hear his heart and mine beating in unison. Tears rolled down my cheeks as I felt his love engulf me. Then I began to sense a sadness. I knew the Lord was weeping for his people, his beloved ones; those chained up and weighed down by hurts. It is the work of the enemy to keep them bound, but God's heart is for us all to know the freedom his truth brings and to fully experience it.

Jesus' words penetrated my heart as he said: "It has been my joy to set you free from the trap of the enemy as you called out to me. I am your Great Redeemer. There are many more who are mine, who need to be released from the snare of the enemy and taste freedom. For too long they have been held back. Now you are free, I have equipped you to help those who are bound. You can speak from your experience, which is the authority I have given you."

Power in unity

Through my tears, I joined in agreement with Jesus and prayed that his people would experience release from bondage and embrace their identity as overcomers in him. I felt truly humbled that I had experienced such a deep connection with Jesus, and that he had shared his heart with me in this wonderful union.

While Jesus was on the earth, he prayed for unity for all believers:

> *I pray also for those who will believe in me through their message, that all of them may be one, Father, just as you are in me and I am in you. May they also be in us so that the world may believe that you have sent me. I have given them the glory that you gave me, that they may be one as we are one – I in them and you in me – so that they may they be brought to complete unity. Then the world will know that you sent me and have loved them even as you have loved me.*
> **(John 17:20-23)**

It is a beautiful thing when we unite as believers and walk in agreement with God. As we abide in him, in a deep relationship of intimacy, we are changed to become more like Jesus. His love fills us and naturally overflows to our brothers and sisters in Christ, and likewise his love for them overflows into our lives.

It is like a harmonious orchestra. We all have our notes to play, and we all make a different sound, but together we create a wonderful symphony as our Conductor brings everything together in his perfect timing. What a glorious, melodious sound we will hear when God's people are in tune with one another and with Christ.

Looking at the world today, we see so much strife and disunity, yet it is Jesus' prayer that the world will see him through his united people. It is from this place of connection that God blesses our lives. This is poetically portrayed in Psalm 133:

How good and pleasant it is
when God's people live together in unity!
It is like precious oil poured on the head,
running down on the beard,
running down on Aaron's beard,
down on the collar of his robe.
It is as if the dew of Hermon
were falling on Mount Zion.
For there the LORD bestows his blessing,
even life for evermore.

My attention was drawn to the "dew of Hermon" mentioned in this psalm, which brought me back to the vision of the mountain. Mount Hermon attracts copious amounts of precipitation, which forms dew in the early morning and evaporates when the sun comes up. The dew keeps the plants watered and the vegetation alive during times of heat and drought.

This is a picture of the Holy Spirit, who refreshes us with his word, sustaining and keeping us alive. And interestingly, it helped to answer a question in my own thinking as to why I often received words first thing in the morning. The formation of dew happens in the early hours, when all is silent. It is in the peace and stillness, when our minds are uncluttered, that we are more attuned to hear the Holy Spirit speaking to us. How vital it is that we hear his still, small, voice, and allow him to guide us and water our lives, in the dry and thirsty land we live in, with the dew of his presence.

Looking at the big picture of the mountain afresh, I could see that it portrayed perfect unity: the mountain of God, with Jesus dancing on the heights and the river of the Holy Spirit flowing down to the valley, bringing God's life everywhere it went.

Opportunities for victory

Every type of difficulty, pain and suffering we experience in life is an opportunity for victory. No pain, no gain; no test, no testimony. Grief shook my life when Peter died. It was absolutely heart-wrenching, but God eventually brought me through to a place of freedom. Would I have chosen this path? No. But I know that God's ways are not always the same as mine, and he has been working something far greater in me than I could have imagined.

None of us like suffering, but it is suffering that produces the type of faith that causes us to overcome. I may have been knocked down for a time, and I wept for many months, but I got back up. My Valley of Baka has taught me to persevere when I could have abandoned all hope. I chose to trust in God, and, as a result of his goodness, he turned every struggle into a blessing. Romans 5:3-5 says:

> *We also glory in our sufferings, because we know that suffering produces perseverance; perseverance, character; and character, hope. And hope does not put us to shame, because God's love has been poured out into our hearts through the Holy Spirit, who has been given to us.*

A double portion

Jesus opened my eyes more and more, until I saw the puzzle pieces of everything he had taken me through over the past year fall into place. Once again, I was drawn to look at Psalm 84, and once again I noticed something different in it. I suddenly saw a "pattern of two" running through the psalm, and I knew that the number two in scripture conveyed union.

There were two birds: the sparrow and the swallow, both finding home near God's altar. Their lessons in sorrow and suffering had brought me great comfort and joy. There were two water sources: the autumn rains and the springs from under the ground. God had poured showers of love over me when my first husband went home to glory. With Peter, I had found myself in the valley and needed to dig for those springs. The two sources of water had finally come together. As I said earlier, it is in the valley that we go from strength to strength. God had strengthened me when I first encountered grief, and now he was strengthening me a second time. I could see my whole life wrapped up in this psalm.

As I pondered the fact that I'd had to walk through the valley of weeping a second time, I heard God say:

> *You have questioned why you suffered grief twice, but know this: you have turned the Valley of Baka into a place of pools; a place of blessing and praise. Now your heart will sing out as you see the wilderness bloom. Twice you have felt weak in grief, but you have gone from strength to strength. Twice we have walked through this valley together, and now I will bestow on you favour and honour, and you will receive a double portion in your land. You will be like a well-watered garden, whose springs never fail.*

Through my grief, God drew me into a deeper unity with him.

He is my beloved, and in him I am fully satisfied. He calls me to the secret place to abide in him, and he awakens my heart to sing. His love makes me bold. In him, I can conquer the valleys and the heights. His love compels me to speak of his goodness, and I want everyone to know of and receive his love. The completed puzzle has revealed his love as a thread that ran through each piece. Nothing can separate me from him. He is forever mine!

Reflection

Ask God to open your spiritual eyes as you spend time with him in prayer. May he give you the Spirit of wisdom and revelation to know him better (Ephesians 1:17), and may you be caught up to the high place, seated with Christ, so that you are able to see the bigger picture. Picture yourself on that mountaintop, looking down on all the problems you're facing right now. Recognise that they are under your feet! This is your place of victory, where you can rest and abide in God.

Prayer

Father, I pray that the eyes of my heart would be flooded with light so I can experience the confident hope to which you have called me: the riches of your glorious inheritance in your people. I am deeply grateful. Amen.

Chapter Thirteen

Letting Go of the Old to Embrace the New

Jesus replied, "No one who puts
his hand to the plough and
looks back is fit for service
in the kingdom of God."
(Luke 9:62)

One morning in February 2022 I woke up feeling troubled in my spirit, having had a short dream about Peter. One moment I was walking down a road with him and the dogs, and then the scene changed and I found myself in an unfamiliar building talking to a lady I didn't know. I told her I needed to phone Peter to let him know where I was, but then the dream abruptly ended.

I am not a huge dreamer, but this one bothered me. I sensed God saying that new life was ahead, but it was time to cut the ties of the past and let go. I sat in bed for a while, catching up on my phone messages. As I did so, I stumbled upon a short YouTube teaching about letting go of the old to embrace the new. The message could not have been any clearer! It was the confirmation I needed to pursue closure.

The previous day I had been fumbling around in the garage, trying to clear some things out. This was the most difficult place to go for me, as it had been Peter's domain. The tools he had used throughout his life as a mechanic were stored inside it. As I glanced around at them, it had felt surreal that he would never use them again.

My mind had been fixed on the task of clearing these tools, which were of no use to me. It had been a difficult day, filled with tears as I thought about all the happy times Peter had spent in his garage, tinkering with his Harley Davidson. It had always been a great joy of his to bring friends and family over and offer them a ride on the back of his bike. Now everything lay still. That old life he had enjoyed was gone.

I knew that if I didn't let go, grief would hold on and anchor me to my past. It was time to move forward into my unknown future. I knew it would be a good one, because I was in safe hands. I also knew that although my earthly life with Peter had ended, he was in glory – and I would see him again for all eternity.

I decided to take positive action. I removed my wedding ring and went down to Peter's garage. This time I opened the door and shouted, "I choose to let go!" several times. It felt good, and it felt right. This was my declaration, and I knew that it had the full power of God in it to release life. Then I closed the garage door as an act of closing the door to the past. I refused to stay trapped in that cycle of grief. Staying in the past was to deny myself the experience of future joy.

My memories of Peter will always be with me, but I knew he would want me to carry on and embrace life. There is a future full of promise ahead, just waiting to be lived. As Paul wrote to the Church in Philippi: "Brothers and sisters, I do not consider myself yet to have taken hold of it. But one thing I do: forgetting what is behind and straining towards what is ahead, I press on towards the goal to win the prize for which God has called me heavenward in Christ Jesus" (Philippians 3:13-14).

I took note of the date: it was the 4th of February 2022. In Hebrew, the number four signifies a door or a path. It can also mean "fullness" or "completion". I marvelled at God's timing, as I knew this was the beginning of his bringing things to completion. The promise of better days ahead had been made, but the timing was in God's hands. I was confident that he would lead me through a new door into a new season. God shuts doors that no one can open, and opens doors that no one can shut.

A light-bearer

It was a glorious April day when I walked the familiar path up to the fields with the dogs. The first signs of spring were beginning to appear. The thorn bushes were in full bloom, festooned with white flowers and bordering the whole length of the field. The abundant blossom was a beautiful sight to behold, and it echoed my sense of impending new life. It had been a year since the vision of Peter handing me into God's care on that very spot. I realised how far I had come since that encounter. God had changed the narrative of my life.

I approached the opening to the thicket, which led into the wood and the open fields beyond. This time my heart was at peace. I gave thanks for Peter's life, honouring all that God had blessed us with. But I knew I was coming out of that season of grieving, and I was looking forward to brighter days ahead. God was restoring me and making all things new. The trauma and pain of those winter months was about to give way to a spring-like joy. The winds of change were blowing the last remnants of ashes away as new life sprang up.

The enemy had fought hard to take me out, but what he had intended for evil, God was turning to good. There was a notable turning from mourning to dancing, from fear to faith, from death to life. I knew that God was going to pay back what I had lost with increase, as this was his promise to me:

> *"Instead of your shame*
> *you will receive a double portion,*
> *and instead of disgrace*
> *you will rejoice in your inheritance.*
> *And so you will inherit a double portion in your land,*
> *and everlasting joy will be yours.*
>
> *For I, the Lord, love justice;*
> *I hate robbery and wrongdoing.*
> *In my faithfulness I will reward my people*
> *and make an everlasting covenant with them."*
> **(Isaiah 61:7-8)**

I grabbed hold of this promise and claimed it for myself. Nothing goes unnoticed by God. He always repays when we have been robbed, because he is a redeeming God. I know that my grief has changed me for the good. I can testify that we are truly in the best hands when we entrust our lives into his keeping. His invitation is simply for us to draw close to him.

Jesus spoke these words to me at this time:

> *Keep your eyes looking forward, because I am taking you into new pastures of harvest and blessing. Be filled with fresh oil every day and*

listen to my instruction. Don't let your past define you or the enemy distract you. To look back is to rob yourself of my blessings for today. It is your present and future that is important, and that is what will bring you fulfilment. Be alert and ready, for there are blessings ahead, but there are also battles ahead. But I have promised you the victory as you stay close to me and walk in obedience. It is my desire for you to win; to become a light-bearer to those around you; to bring glory to my name.

Dancing on the waves

At the end of April, my whole family went away for a week's holiday by the sea. It was just what we all needed to recover from the hard winter months. I spent a full day on the beach, looking out at the waves as they rolled in. They mirrored the sense of freedom and space I felt in my spirit. I put on my headset and listened to worship music as I gazed out to sea. I suddenly saw myself dancing on the waves and heard God say that the waves and breakers of grief would not keep sweeping over, taking me to the ground, but that I would be dancing on top of them with triumphant joy.

A month later I met up with a friend and shared what I had seen on the beach that day. She asked me if I had heard the song "Dancing on the Waves". I hadn't, but I listened to the words carefully, thankful that God was giving me his song once again. The words echoed what I had seen, only it wasn't just me dancing on the waves. Jesus was dancing with me.

A written memorial

The death of Moses signalled the end of Israel's wanderings in the wilderness. The people grieved his passing for a period, then God appointed Joshua to take Israel across the River Jordan into a new future. In Joshua 3, the priests carried the Ark of the Covenant ahead of the people, and when their feet touched the edge of the Jordan its waters stopped flowing from upstream and piled up in a heap, allowing the people to cross on dry ground. Israel had entered a new future of unchartered paths.

In Joshua 4, we read about stones collected from the riverbed, which were constructed into a monument as a memorial for all that God had done. As far as I am concerned, the writing of this book is my memorial to mark all that God has carried me through during my journey of grief. It is also a memorial to Jean-Paul and to Peter, both of whom shaped my life and our family, leaving their mark of love on us all.

In 1 Peter 2:4-5, God's people are referred to as "living stones":

> *As you come to him, the living Stone – rejected by humans but chosen by God and precious to him – you also, like living stones, are being built into a spiritual house to be a holy priesthood, offering spiritual sacrifices acceptable to God through Jesus Christ.*

We are living stones, put together to memorialise God, and we are living testimonies to his goodness. Our stories will live on throughout eternity to the praise of his glory.

It goes without saying that 2021-2022 was devastating for me, being parted from Peter, but it was also the most profound of my life. Grief broke my heart, but God rooted me in his steadfast love and established me on a sure foundation that would not collapse. He revealed his love for me through the sparrow;

nurturing me when I was broken and in shock. Through the swallow, God delivered me from my restless wanderings. He filled me with peace and rest at his altar of healing, and it was at this stage that my book was birthed.

Throughout the journey, the dove – the blessed Holy Spirit – mourned with me. He ministered his comfort and drew me closer to him. This was when I realised that nothing can be of any earthly effect until we wholeheartedly surrender to his gracious leading. God also spoke to me through the raven, assuring me that he would be my supply, so I need not worry. As I waited and sat at his feet, he renewed my strength to rise up on eagles' wings and soar in his presence. I was so thankful to God for that. My sorrow became the source of God's blessing. He turns every broken situation around for his and our good. And he gives us everything we need to walk through grief into triumph.

Reflection

God communicated his heart to me through these five birds. He will speak to you in diverse and personally relevant ways if you simply open your eyes and look around. Creation is a powerful tool that he will use to speak to you.

Ask God to give you clear vision, and may your spiritual senses be awakened to a whole new world around you. He wants to reveal his heart to you, especially if you are going through a time of grief. You are so special to him, and he is right by your side, holding your hand. Your journey is unique, and God has a perfect plan for your healing. He will reveal himself to you and speak words of comfort and encouragement over you. Look for him and you will find him. Then rest in his loving embrace.

Prayer (for those who are grieving)

Father, you are my ever-present help in times of trouble. I run into your arms, because my life is broken with grief and my heart is filled with sorrow. I cannot offer you anything except my tears. Holy Spirit, comfort me with your love and shelter me from this storm. Forgive me for my past mistakes and wash me with your blood. Give me a renewed hope that one day I will experience your abundant life and rejoice again. Amen.

Acknowledgements

Thank you, Joy Tibbs, for your thorough edits, bringing clarity to my sentences and provoking me with your questioning comments to draw out the best in me. It has been an education!

Thanks to my pastor Ryan Morton and wife Sarah for your love and prayers at a time when I found it difficult to face going to church. You have always encouraged and supported me, and allowed me the space I needed to heal.

To Brenda Hucker and Graham Brown for proofreading my book while it was still being developed. Your words inspired me to keep going.

Thanks to Michael and Jan Bryant of MB Ministries, whose online broadcasts brought revelation and encounter with God that encouraged and strengthened me in my grief. When I was down, God met me on the meadow to restore my soul.

To my dear friend Tina Cooke. I would have felt like giving up had you not been there. Thank you for bringing life and love into the pain of grief. Our dog walks in the park together have been precious and healing – a touch of heaven!

To all my girl friends who have prayed, rung me and rallied round. You are an amazing troop, a force to be reckoned with, and I thank God for the precious gift of our friendship

To my children for their support, love and resilience to keep going despite the challenges you have had to face from a young age. Your dads would be so proud of you, as am I. Keep your eyes on Jesus. He is the answer, through and through. I love you all so very much.

Most importantly, I give thanks to my God and Saviour, Jesus Christ, who has my heart completely, and whose love astounds me. You never give up on me, your arms are strong and comforting, and I want to bring you glory in all that I do.